Questioning Library Neutrality

Essays from Progressive Librarian

Questioning Library Neutrality

Essays from Progressive Librarian

Edited by Alison Lewis

Library Juice Press
Duluth, Minnesota

Copyright held by authors of respective articles, from dates of original publication, as indicated in the text.

Published in 2008.

Library Juice Press
P.O. Box 3320
Duluth, MN 55803
http://libraryjuicepress.com/

Library Juice Press is an imprint of Litwin Books, LLC.

This books is printed on acid-free paper that meets all present ANSI standards for archival preservation.

Library of Congress Cataloging-in-Publication Data

Questioning library neutrality : essays from Progressive librarian / edited by Alison Lewis.
   p. cm.
  Includes bibliographical references.
  ISBN 978-0-9778617-7-4 (acid-free paper)
  1. Libraries and society. 2. Library science--Political aspects. 3. Library science--Social aspects. 4. Library science--Moral and ethical aspects. 5. Librarians--Professional ethics. 6. Libraries--Censorship. I. Lewis, Alison M., 1959- II. Progressive librarian.
  Z716.4.Q47 2008
  021.2--dc22
                            2007046352

CONTENTS

Introduction, by Alison Lewis	1.
Politics and Anti-Politics in Librarianship, by Mark Rosenzweig	5.
Corporate Inroads in Librarianship: The Fight for the Soul of the Profession in the New Millenium, by Peter Mcdonald	9.
Librarianship and Resistance, by Sandy Iverson	25.
A Few Gates Redux: An Examination of the Social Responsibilities Debate in the Early 1970s and 1990s, by Steven Joyce	33.
Activist Librarianship: Heritage or Heresy? by Ann Sparanese	67.
Activist Librarianship Bibliography, by Ann Sparanese	83.
The Myth of the Neutral Professional, by Robert Jensen	89.
Information Criticism: Where is It? by Jack Andersen	97.
Towards Self-Reflection in Librarianship: What is Praxis? by John J. Doherty	109.
The Professional is Political: Redefining the Social Role of Public Libraries, by Shiraz Durrani and Elizabeth Smallwood	119.
The Hottest Place in Hell: The Crisis of Neutrality in Contemporary Librarianship, by Joseph Good	141.
About the Contributors	147.

Questioning Neutrality: An Introduction

By Alison M. Lewis

Why, here at the beginning of the twenty-first century, are we putting together a volume of papers that question the role of neutrality within librarianship? In fact, why question neutrality at all? Isn't it a positive quality, one of the hallmarks of our professionalism as librarians?

Certainly it has been seen as a virtue among librarians that we do not allow ourselves to be driven solely by our own viewpoints, but rather strive to make available to library patrons a range of information sources covering a variety of opinions and ideas. In my own experience doing collection development in political science, for example, I've bought books by Noam Chomsky and by Ann Coulter—and by just about everyone else in between. And while I'd personally prefer to read Chomsky, I bought books by Coulter because I knew there was an interest in and a demand for them. Because I have a strong belief in intellectual freedom, I had no desire to suppress Coulter's ideas even though I do not agree with them. Historically, libraries have been one of the places where citizens can be exposed to a variety of viewpoints, including unpopular or minority views. In our democratic society, this has been held up as a public good. Access provided by libraries to materials on racial equality and women's rights, for example, have helped provide fertile ground for moving such ideas from the fringe to the mainstream.

This is well and good, but we soon find ourselves on a very slippery slope. The Library Bill of Rights, Article 2 states that "Libraries should provide materials and information presenting all points of view on current and historical issues." As I write, in the sixth year of the quagmire of the Iraq War, I wonder if it is humanly possible to present *all* points of view on the war and what is to be done about it? No two people seem to express the same opinion on the topic, and the situation (and viewpoints along with it) changes weekly, if not daily. While we can strive to present a *range* of opinions and views on the war, the word "all" in the Library Bill of Rights statement is an impossible goal, dooming librarians to failure in following its dictates. "All" is a word generally to be avoided, along with "always" and "never," because they too often lead to overgeneralization and therefore, to untruth.

If we were somehow able to make available all viewpoints, or failing that, a healthy range of viewpoints, should we consider each of these viewpoints equally valid and deserving of equal amounts of shelf space and budget dollars? I also write at a time when a number of school boards and libraries find themselves under pressure from some religious groups to "equally" provide access to teaching and materials on the theory of creationism or intelligent design, as is already provided for the theory of evolution. And what about viewpoints expressing Neo-Nazi ideology or Holocaust denial? Do these deserve equal representation along with historical studies of World War II and personal stories of Holocaust survivors? Am I not a hypocrite for failing to enthusiastically embrace these "minority" viewpoints, given that I've already glowingly referred to libraries' earlier role in providing access to "fringe" viewpoints on racial equality and women's rights?

The adage that "Everybody is entitled to their own opinions, but not to their own facts" is usually attributed to the late U.S. Senator Daniel Patrick Moynihan, has some bearing here. I would certainly advocate including books on creationism and intelligent design in just about any library collection, not only for those whose faith leads them to consider these the "right" viewpoint, but also for those who strive to learn more about the ideas held by these groups in order to better refute them. Likewise, I would include some representation of neo-Nazi or Holocaust denial materials in an adult library collection, in order to understand their arguments and be better prepared to argue against them. But creationism and Holocaust denial have been discredited by the vast majority of the scientists and historians, respectively. They don't hold equal weight in the marketplace of ideas, and they are not deserving of an equal share of limited library resources.

It has already been "discovered" by particle physicists, anthropologists, and a range of other researchers, that it is impossible to be neutral. Even if it were possible for me to wash away all influences that sway me in a particular direction, I would not want to achieve that state of neutrality. From a moral standpoint, I have no desire to remain neutral when faced with a choice between science based on the scientific method or science based on theology, and between historical fact or hate speech. To hide behind the idea of "neutrality" in such instances is to be party to promulgating misinformation or worse.

Interestingly enough, it has been library administrators enamored of the business model of librarianship who have most visibly been abandoning the idea of "neutrality," at least where their own libraries are concerned. Funding has gotten so tight for all libraries and use patterns have changed so significantly over the past few years that no library is able to rest on its laurels as a public or institutional "good" and expect to survive. Administrators know that it is a matter of survival to become advocates rather than neutral bystanders, and that it is necessary for them to promote and even "market" and "sell" their library's services. As an educator of future librarians, I wish that this sense of advocacy extended beyond the individual library to the profession itself. I am continuously disheartened by the lack of understanding of or support for libraries and librarians in the larger society. Underfunding and deprofessionalization are two symptoms of a potentially fatal illness within the library profession.

For these reasons and more, it seems past the time to present a work focused on the concept of "neutrality" within librarianship. The essays that follow all relate to neutrality in a philosophical or practical sense, and sometimes both. They are a selection of essays originally published in *Progressive Librarian*, the journal of the Progressive Librarians Guild, and they are presented in the chronological order of their appearance there.

We begin with *Progressive Librarian* editor Mark Rosenzweig's editorial, "Politics and Anti-Politics," which provides a philosophical framework for considering the historical role of "neutrality" within the profession of librarianship. It is followed by Peter McDonald's "Corporate Inroads and Librarianship," which exposes the outsourcing of library functions in various settings and advocates for the retention of local professional involvement and humanistic values. Sandy Iverson provides a post-modernist and feminist critique of neutrality or "objectivity" in "Librarianship and Resistance." Steven Joyce revisits the so-called "Berninghausen debate" surrounding issues of social responsibilities within the American Library Association in the 1970s and relates it to a similar conflict within the profession over homosexuality in the 1990s in "A Few Gates Redux." In "Activist Librarianship: Heritage or Heresy?" Ann Sparanese relates the circumstances surrounding her now-famous "saving" of Michael Moore's book *Stupid White Men* and the motivations behind her own decision to act rather than remain a passive, neutral observer. Robert Jensen provides useful insights into the impossibility of remaining neutral with his comparison of librarians to professionals working in journalism and higher education in "The Myth of the Neutral Professional." Jack Andersen's "Information Criticism: Where is It?" looks at librarianship's inability to critique and analyze the information it deals with and places the blame for this on the profession's embrace of a technological and managerial discourse that overlooks practical use and societal impact. Likewise, John Doherty challenges librarianship's lack of critical self-awareness in "Towards Self-Reflection in Librarianship: What is Praxis?" and provides practical examples of his own attempts to integrate the ideas of educational theorists into his practice of bibliographic instruction. In "The Professional is Political," Shiraz Durrani and Elizabeth Smallwood examine the library within a global context, then narrow their focus to innovative practices in public libraries in Britain, providing a concrete example of a needs-based youth advocacy program. Lastly, Joseph Good critiques neutrality as a form of moral relativism in "The Hottest Place in Hell."

Here at the beginning of the twenty-first century, "neutrality" no longer means "impartiality" or "objectivity," but too often lapses into what might be better termed "indifference." These essays are presented in the hope that they will stimulate further interest in and debate about the concept of neutrality within the library community, if not provoking the downright opposite of indifference.

Politics and Anti-Politics in Librarianship

By Mark Rosenzweig

Most American librarians today take it for granted that our profession stands for the unequivocal defense of intellectual freedom, freedom of speech, and a number of other very fine principles. It is surely among the best things about us that we now see ourselves as being almost definitionally committed to democratic values. But in the last decades we have perhaps grown too used to casting our profession in this heroic mold, as if historically it has always been true that librarians as a profession and *en masse* have opposed censorship, bigotry, and intolerance and held tenaciously to intellectual freedom as our cardinal professional value.

This static image of librarianship is, however, a myth (comforting though it might be), as any objective examination of library history would demonstrate. Those who take it as reality are likely to lose sight not just of where we've come from but of how we must proceed. Among those who apparently take the myth for the reality are librarians who are presently railing against the intrusion of "politics" and the destruction of "neutrality" in American Library Association (ALA), provoked by the recent (barely successful) effort to get the association to take a stand against the Persian Gulf War and the censorship it would inevitably entail, as if this were a betrayal of our traditions and of timeless professional values.

History, however, reminds us, with regards to neutrality, that the very emergence of the library profession was intimately associated with ideologically-informed efforts to place the whole development of education and mass enlightenment under the aegis of elite business interests. These interests envisaged systems of rationalized schools and libraries as powerful instruments of social integration and control, and our profession consciously placed itself at the service of this eminently ideological project. This is not, of course, to say that the organization of libraries in the public sphere in this era—which was the great impetus to the development of the entire profession—did not have a significance which transcended these ideological limits. It certainly represented a potential extension of democracy for masses of Americans. But we would do well to remember that if libraries as institutions implicitly opened democratic vistas, our librarian predecessors were hardly democratic in their overt professional attitude or mission, being primarily concerned with the regulation of literacy, the policing of literary taste, and the propagation of a particular class culture with all its political, economic, and social prejudices.

In fact, the idea of the neutrality of librarianship, so enshrined in today's library ideology (and so often read back into the indefinite past) was alien to these earlier generations. The origins of the ideas of impartiality and neutrality, which come to fruition much later, are perhaps more connected to the historical process of institutional rationalization and bureaucratization (of which the new librarians were enthusiastic exponents) than to a preoccupation with intellectual freedom. If we have become more democratic, more concerned with equity and social justice, it has been because of a political process and not because of a hewing to imaginary first principles of neutrality.

No fair historical examination of librarianship in America could fail to note as well that its annals are replete with examples of partisanship, albeit not necessarily (as one would like to believe) of free thought or the rights of minorities, but too often of the causes of the powers-that-be and the forces of order, sometimes taking the form of a passive defense of the status quo, sometimes taking shape as an active campaign for a new cause.

It is no secret, for example, that in seeking recognition of its identity and acknowledgment of its importance the profession energetically curried favor with business and government by actively endorsing World War I. Libraries were made veritable instruments of propaganda with librarians zealously weeding and censoring all unpatriotic material, promoting pro-war views, and persecuting antiwar librarians. What precluded librarians being anti-war? Not an aversion to politics!

During the witchhunts of the fifties, didn't librarians at New York Public Library (and elsewhere) dutifully remove the books of blacklisted authors from the shelves (though supposedly putting them in storage rather than burning them as librarians in other countries might not have been loath to do)? This cowardly political act was considered consistent with the prevailing notion of professional responsibility. Who can say politics has been alien to librarianship? But did they have to be those politics?

If we are inclined to believe that we have completely overcome our "political" past, we should consider that many ALA members are fighting against implementation of a poor people's policy, that there is resistance at the highest level to discussing censorship in Israel, that effective action against South African apartheid was blocked by ALA Council, and only months ago our association turned a blind eye to members who censored material going to troops in the Persian Gulf.

The question, as a glance at our history reveals, is not whether politics enters into professional matters (it always has), but rather what politics, and to what effect. We should remember too that it was only since the 1960s, largely under the political impetus of activist librarians fighting for a substantive (rather than merely formal/legal) concept of intellectual freedom based on engagement with civil and human rights issues and a politicized sense of social responsibility, that the notion of our commitment to democratic values has been moved to the central place in librarianship and given the expanded meaning we are all apt to take for granted today. It may be convenient for some librarians to ignore or forget all this and assert that politics has no place in our profession, but such a view can only be predicated on historical amnesia. As the chilling specter of a campaign against the fashionable bogey of "political correctness" descends on ALA, the Progressive Librarians Guild (PLG) maintains that every new problem which arises, whether it has to do with a new technology or responses to a new social crisis, involves questions of the library's relations to the rest of society which cannot but have a political dimension. Every such problem challenges us to live up to our sometimes all too complacently assumed and (despite our rhetoric) sometimes rather tenuous commitment to democratic values. Any stifling of political debate in the name of an ahistorical notion of professionalism would mean not the suppression of divisive politics, but only the unthinking acceptance of a particular politics.

[Note: "Politics and Anti-Politics in Librarianship" originally appeared *Progressive Librarian,* No. 3, Summer, 1991.]

Corporate Inroads and Librarianship: The Fight for the Soul of the Profession in the New Millennium

By Peter McDonald

At heart, censorship is all about choice. In the United States, the freedom to choose what we want to see, hear, and read is granted as a right by our Constitution, which specifically protects these rights from government or external interference. In the smaller sphere of our profession, much of the censorship debate focus rests on issues attending the high-profile banning of books and the muzzling of risqué ideas. Since these are rights granted to us by the First Amendment, and are specifically identified in our "Library Bill of Rights," to its credit, our profession has often been in the forefront, championing our Right to Read in equally high profile litigations.

But if this were the only, or even primary, measure of censorship faced by our culture, the issues and implications of the debate would be easier to untangle, if not in the courts than certainly with our wallets. After all, in most locales, we can buy the banned book and have done with it. In short, the common discussion of censorship as portrayed in the mainstream media does not really explore the underlying factors that contribute to censorship. It is too often simplistically framed and fails utterly to probe into the abiding consolidation and hegemony in media production facing our democracy. What we get instead is a sound bite portraying a struggle of opposing, yet in some mysterious way, equally valid ideas, with merits and human drama on both sides! Gays vs. The Christian Right, and so forth. These imbroglios gain wide notoriety not because they are particularly intractable or menacing in and of themselves, but because the corporate structure which defines these "censorship" debates in the media, clearly wants the focus of the discussion to remain glued to these diverting phenomena and not, as will be addressed in this article, on the structure of corporate hegemony itself. Plainly put, how does a free and informed citizenry remain so, when the entire structure of our society is permeated to its core by the paradigm of corporate hegemony, a power which indeed dominates most aspects of our lives? Since multinational corporations overwhelmingly control what it is we see, hear, and read, avenues by which a democratic society might logically inform itself, where do we go to step outside this dominant exemplar to find an unbiased corpus of ideas untainted by the cynical values of the marketplace?

One logical place to go, of course, and one of the few remaining openly civic spaces remaining in our harried world, is the public library, a place which we can only hope offers access to published material infused with humanistic, environmental, and people-centered world views. Unfortunately, this, too, is a simplistic description. For it will be the task of this inquiry to show that this Norman Rockwell impression of the public library (and academic ones, too, for that matter) as a civic forum of free inquiry, is slowly and systematically being co-opted by the same models of corporate management which the libraries of our nation once prided themselves on keeping at arm's length.

I argue that it is precisely this corporate hegemony which systematically squelches free expression in art, culture, information access, and yes, by extension, also in librarianship itself. This surely is the real fulcrum of the censorship debate. The greatest threat to our experiencing the fullness of our First Amendment rights comes not from noisy cabals of incensed zealots bent on banning books, but rather from corporate America itself where "choice" becomes nothing more than another commodity marketed like any other—stream-lined, made safe, and sold like a sugary confection to the masses a la Wal-Mart. Arguably, financial bottom lines (it won't sell), self protection (beware the labor movement/social issues), and an equally palpable fear of controversy (why stir up trouble?) are the core reasons corporations stifle the unfettered flow of challenging ideas which might otherwise "shock" our collective sensibilities to action. True this is most apparent on television and cable programming, with its tapioca sitcoms, dramas and reality shows, but it creeps into the print domain as well. But without that unfettered flow, the democratizing debate of true citizenship is handicapped at the outset. As a citizenry, we then suffer the consequences of this consolidated access to ideas. We see this in the opaque tyranny of technology, which bamboozles us into believing that the glut of "information" brought to our computer screens at ever faster speeds of gadgetry, somehow makes up for the increasing dearth in the breadth and depth of what is being offered. This is the false algorithm of the Information Age which states: more information + faster access = more choice! Librarians for the most part no more question this nod to the "bottom line" of our pervasive corporatism than they do the technological wizardry which defines it. In this cozy acceptance of the status quo lies a much more insidious corporate dominance which has the potential to deaden the very soul of our profession.

Naturally, the censorship of unfettered ideas also has analogies in the cut-throat marketing of common goods. At first blush, the marketing strategies of large corporations may seem to take us a long way from the matter at hand. Public and academic libraries, after all, pride themselves in the abstract on their independence from the corporate structures and the profit-seeking dictums which drive the private sector. However, upon closer examination, there is arguably not a single task accomplished in our modern library systems which is not directly or indirectly dominated by external corporate decision making. This is hardly news to librarians who are members of the American Library Association (ALA)'s Social Responsibilities Round Table (SRRT) or the Progressive Librarians Guild (PLG). This small cadre of "conscientious objectors" is but a drop in the bucket when one considers the extent to which the general membership of ALA has intertwined its operations and organizational goals with those of multi-million dollar corporations such as EBSCO, Reed-Elsevier, Meckler Media, and Ameritech.

If, as has been argued, censorship is at heart a matter of free choice, free of corporate meddling and zealous restriction, a brief detour to the local supermarket might be instructive. This is not as far-fetched as might at first be construed. Consider for a moment the sheer unending volume of products for sale on the shelves of the supermarket nearest you. Among corporate apologists, this is evidence that the public is always given a "choice" by the mechanisms of "free enterprise" which happily supply this plethora of goods. After all, if the average shopper can "choose" between forty-eight brands of breakfast cereal stacked on the shelves, surely they have the right to make their "choice" with their wallets! The consumer, in fact, is given no choice with this shabby simulacrum because 90% of the cereals on major supermarket shelves are produced by just one or two huge conglomerates (General Mills and Kellogg). The clear intention of these corporations is to use their size and financial muscle to demand of every supermarket chain with which they do business that the supermarket must also buy the forty-seven other bogus brands of cereals offered by the company. Nutritionists have proven these are virtually indistinguishable food stuffs (grain, sugar, salt, and food coloring) which have simply been shaped, colored, and packaged differently by product wizards in sales departments in order for the conglomerate to flood the allotted shelf space with its own volume of wares. Flood the shelves and the competitors, especially small competitors, are denied any chance at a market share.

Naturally, any sensible supermarket chain out to make a profit for itself will agree to this bullying scam for reasons too obvious and numerous to describe here. But the strategic intentions of agribusiness are perfectly apparent. Corporate bullying (or in the imaginary parlance of pundits this "good marketing strategy by a corporate leader in the field") virtually eliminates from supermarket shelves breakfast cereals from smaller wholesalers offering organic foods or locally produced granolas, or non-traditional grain products and so on. These latter offerings are closer to a real choice, of course, because they empower local control of the economy; yet to a citizenry self-servingly uninformed, the sham stacks of forty-eight brands of cereals are so easily swallowed as "choice" precisely because they "look" so different. No wonder corporations get away with the things they do. Besides, to demand real variety and choice would mean bothering to take the time to demand of the supermarket manager that you want the off-beat products which were elbowed out of the way by those Sugar Puff and Frankenberry boxes. So much easier to grab brand X and get on with your busy day!

It is a sad fact, but librarianship today suffers from this same miasma of false "choice" as does the rest of society. At all levels of the profession, there seems to be a growing lack of critical self-examination of what corporate inroads into our service means, notably when librarians make their management decisions but leave corporate-dominated assumptions unexamined. Like Janus, this peculiar self-censorship has many faces which merely vary to greater or lesser extent in their level of insidiousness. And all facets of the profession are prone. From collection development, to discarding aging card catalogs in favor of OPACs, to corporate sponsored symposia for librarians, to installing expensive digital technologies, corporations increasingly call the shots on how libraries do their business and provide access to users.

One area where this willingness to accept corporate-dominated information is plainly and uncritically evident lies in the selection process of collection development officers seen in most libraries. For example, studies have shown that most collection development selectors rely on the major, commercial book review journals—*Booklist*, *Choice*, *Library Journal*, and *Publishers Weekly*, to make their materials selection choices —55% of the time, apparently, with publishers catalogs a distant 24% (Serebnick, 1992). While not an insidious statistic in and of itself, other studies have shown that these highly influential journals consistently review the output of big publishers compared to small presses by a ratio of almost 18 to 1 (Cullars, 1984). It hardly needs emphasizing, but recall that small presses, to their credit, consistently provide alternate viewpoints which push against the current of acceptable opinion, publishing ideas and controversial material rarely found in the catalogs and book lists of major commercial publishers. But the likelihood of their being added to library collections against odds of 18 to 1 is at best problematic, and in reality, disheartening since they are marginalized at selection source and are sometimes pooh-poohed in the mainstream journals' reviews. Furthermore, as cost-cutting trends accelerate at both public and academic libraries, shared cataloging becomes the norm through computerized nationwide systems such as OCLC. With so few small press titles being processed to begin with, acquisition decisions are often adversely affected due to lack of an existing online record. The small press book is simply not purchased for lack of an existing record or a Library of Congress Cataloging-in-Publication (CIP) record (Lee, 1995). Internal library costs to provide original cataloguing, a service many smaller libraries cannot afford, nixes the purchase at source.

Elsewhere, in a polemic article published several years ago in *The New Yorker* (1994), Nicholson Baker argued convincingly that the online public catalogs of our major libraries are increasingly becoming little more than mirror images of one another, a pale reflection of the rich heritage of our written culture, with only selected and highly prized collections differentiating these "access points." Naturally, the quirky depth and often serendipitous breadth of the old card catalog, which reflected the unique holdings of a particular library, has been universally superseded by the aseptic wonder of the commercially engineered, painfully literal, electronic catalog which looks unremittingly the same whether you are at a workstation at Yale University or at a terminal at the Tacoma Public Library half a continent away. In short, libraries are mimicking the corporate tendency to streamline operations in the name of budgetary efficiency and faster access.

Is this a creeping corporate form of self-imposed censorship? Certainly. Inherent in these time-saving, faster-access, print-on-demand technologies are barely hidden agendas and structures of power which consistently uphold the highest denominator of the status quo. Not so long ago, for example, the charge of the Government Printing Office and other federal information repositories was to publish free of charge (or at minimal cost), the full array of documents pertaining to national governance in the broadest sense of our democracy. Flawed as this system may have been, it was certainly a cut above the current politically-motivated trend to outsource government documents to commercial vendors who then offer these same federal documents our tax dollars originally produced back to us electronically at exorbitant (sometimes at per-minute online) prices. Nowadays, if you don't have cash wads in pocket or a handy $2000 computer lying around, accessing federal publications can be a daunting challenge, especially for the disenfranchised and the poor. It has become so costly, in fact, that many libraries now charge their users for this service (Chaffee, 1995).

An anecdotal observation here might be instructive. Recently, there was a contentious debate among science selectors (to which this author was party) as to whether Cornell University should join the members of its consortia (NERL, the Northeast Research Libraries Network) and collectively sign a contract with Academic Press for on-line access to an important selection of their science e-journals. From the outset, there was a vocal faction (suffering from that common library ailment, "bandwagonitis"), who espoused the morbid fear held by many librarians that institutions not hell-bent for online access might be left in the dark ages of print, while sister institutions basked in the new dawn of a nascent "virtual library." Be this as it may, to the credit of the majority of Cornell science selectors, the contract with Academic was spurned outright for it placed the powers of access and preservation of the journals in the hands of a commercial publisher which apparently had no real idea how it would retain its market share or increase its profits in this emerging online environment. Still less guarantee long-term stewardship of the digital product. A variety of hobbled pay schemes and access mechanisms were hastily thrown together as the negotiations between NERL and Academic unfolded. The final contract proffered was little more than a muddled shot in the dark, for it stipulated, in part, that retention of print copies had to coexist with the purchase of online access for a period of three years. This essentially increased the cost for the same material (now in separate formats) by something close to 30%. To the selectors' way of thinking, this gave Academic Press an unearned windfall in revenues as well as the right to dictate how the selectors would go about their collection duties by tying their hands to retain titles they might otherwise choose to cancel. To its credit, Cornell stood alone against the contract and NERL, when the latter signed with Academic Press despite the contract's obvious shortcomings. Nevertheless, one librarian responsible for collections at a sister Ivy League institution crowed via e-mail: "Signing this contract, brings us to the threshold of instigating the virtual library of the future!" This is the key slogan of bandwagonitis as it pertains to technology: To be *au currant*, friends, you gotta have it!

The apotheosis of this trend of signing away autonomy to corporate interests in the name of the "library of the future," came this past autumn, when Hawaii State Librarian Bart Kane peremptorily decided to provide an $11.2 million system-wide outsourcing contract to mega-wholesaler Baker & Taylor (B&T), one of the biggest corporate book vendors in the field. By this single action, Kane handed over selection, acquisitions, cataloging, and processing for all public libraries in the state of Hawaii to an unaffiliated, publicly unaccountable corporation with no integral ties to the citizens of Hawaii. According to *School Library Journal* (1996), Kane's "decision to shift selection to a vendor was necessary to comply with the governor's request for deep budget cuts." This is the tired argument of the bureaucrat, a familiar ruse often used by library administrators to justify cuts in service in order to provide, among other things, access to streamlined electronic resources which are usually exorbitantly expensive. Excellent articles by Celeste West (1983) and John Buschman (1994) handily refute this old chestnut of justifying all sorts of management shenanigans in the name of budget cuts in their respective articles on library censorship.

As for Baker and Taylor, they have defended themselves, in part, by stressing that they have over 18,000 publishers' addresses on file and can readily provide the breadth of material necessary to accommodate the "Aloha State's" gamut of reading tastes. But a 1988 study of B&T, indicated that "the top 200 commercial publishers account for 90% of Baker and Taylor's business. The top 50 publishers account for 80%" (Mutter, 1998). In other words, of their 18,000 publishers on file, "choice" to B&T really means the top 50 commercial publishers with whom they have cozy and ongoing accounts. To any thinking Hawaiian this must be a troubling statistic indeed, notably so since Hawaii itself has a thriving cottage industry of small presses which must now compete with the entrenched accounts of B&T's big mainland publishers. Relationships between these small local presses and front library staff, cultivated over decades, have summarily been lost to corporate streamlining in the wake of Kane's decision. Indeed, e-mails posted by disaffected selectors within the Hawaiian state library system, clearly show that their worst fears have materialized (Carpenter, 1997).

Obviously, Baker & Taylor have not lived up to their promise to provide the breadth and depth of locally meaningful material to Hawaiian state libraries, and recent discussions on the matter on the PLGNet-L listserv have revealed that B&T's actual contract is worded in such a way as to make the mega-vendor virtually unaccountable for its shoddy materials selection no matter how egregious its behavior. In a rear-guard action to bring attention to this matter, the Librarians Association of Hawaii has specifically asked that the B&T contract be audited (as noted in a *Honolulu Advertiser* article on a hearing before the Hawaii State Supreme Court). Worse yet, there is a clause in the B&T contract which states: "The STATE acknowledges and agrees that the Performance Targets set forth in Exhibit B attached hereto and made a part hereof are target goals only and Contractor's failure to achieve any or all of them will not constitute an Event of Default." Sound familiar? The author at press time was not able to obtain a copy of "Exhibit B", but the gist of the clause, in any case, is clear. As one recent e-mail posted to PLGNet-L stated: "B&T therefore has been left off the hook" (Tomioka, 1997).

Then in October last year, Hawaii state library staff received a memo from their central administration forbidding them from using internal e-mail to air their views on this matter or to discuss the issues and implications of the B&T contract (Denwall, n.d.).

Where was ALA's vaunted championing of First Amendment rights on this restrictive dictum? There was none, at least not from the Association at large or from its Chicago offices. To its credit, the Alternatives in Print Task Force of ALA sponsored a program on the issue at the ALA mid-winter conference in Washington, D.C. in February of 1997. But this was at best a pallid reprimand of State Librarian Bart Kane et al's peremptory behavior. If this is the extent of ALA's moral muscle, let alone of its outrage at censorship within its own ranks, what hope for the profession at large?

In an additional instance the e-mail message quoted here was sent out to the world from OCLC headquarters on January 16, 1997 from Marifay Makssour:

OCLC, ACADEMIC BOOK CENTER, SOLINET TO PROVIDE AUTOMATED COLLECTION AND TECHNICAL SERVICES TO NEW FLORIDA UNIVERSITY

OCLC, Academic Book Center and the Southeastern Library Network (SOLINET) will provide automated collection and technical services to the library at the Florida Gulf Coast University, Florida's 10th and newest state university, which is scheduled to open in August 1997.

Under the unique two-year agreement, OCLC and Academic Book Center will provide a fully cataloged, shelf-ready, opening-day collection, as well as ongoing collection development, acquisitions, cataloging, authority control, physical processing and fund accounting. SOLINET will provide training and support.

"Our library has embarked on a bold, new approach where the collection and technical services operation is completely outsourced from day one," said Carolyn Gray, Dean of Library Services at Florida Gulf Coast University. "Our objective is to provide fully cataloged books and materials that support the university's curriculum and that minimize physical handling by library staff.

"By outsourcing our book purchasing to Academic Book Center and our technical processing functions to OCLC, we can accomplish this goal and focus our limited resources on direct delivery of high quality, customized library services to students and faculty," Dr. Gray said.

Thus the Library of the Future in this brave new model will apparently have all collection and technical processing functions outsourced from day one. The ever present OCLC, by the way, was originally chartered by member libraries as a not-for-profit organization to assist in the creation of an online union catalog of members' holdings. "In 1967, the presidents of the colleges and universities in the state of Ohio founded the Ohio College Library Center (OCLC) to develop a computerized system in which the libraries of Ohio academic institutions could share resources and reduce costs" (OCLC, n.d.). What started out as a modest mid-western collaboration between a handful of public and academic libraries, has become today Online Computer Library Center, Inc., a corporate-dominated behemoth whose structure, governance, and business practices are indistinguishable from any Fortune 500 company. Here in a nutshell lies the dilemma we are addressing: that a truly nonprofit library consortia evolved into a world a giant in every way mimicking a transnational corporation which has had to defend its "nonprofit" status in both the press and the courts. The direction our profession is headed is made abundantly clear in all these instances.

The American Library Association's Code of Professional Ethics unambiguously states that ALA members are "explicitly committed to intellectual freedom and the freedom of access to information." Furthermore, they must resist "all efforts by groups or individuals to censor library materials." These are high sounding words, and were doubtless penned in good faith when first codified. But what becomes of that vaunted "access to information" when the very mechanisms of access, namely our computers, our databases, our networks are wholly corporate designed and in the case of many databases, wholly created and priced for commercial gain? Little wonder that among the 600 odd databases available via Knight-Ridder's DIALOG system, not one is alternative or progressive in nature. Ditto Nexis and Lexis. This comes as no big surprise. These systems were not designed to inform a concerned citizenry, they were marketed expressly for business and legal enterprises, and only incidentally for libraries. And even not-for-profit databases such as AGRICOLA (agriculture) and MEDLINE (medicine) are dominated by the ethics and practices of the status quo, in this case by mainstream science and big medicine respectively. Little wonder that agricultural systems such as organic cultivation of crops and alternative medicinal practices such as homeopathy or even chiropractic receive such short shrift, forming a mere fraction of the bibliographic citations of the whole (less than 2%) in both databases. There is probably no consciously nefarious intent here by the collaborators who compile these databases, since both MEDLINE and AGRICOLA are federally funded enterprises produced by federally funded libraries. But both the National Library of Medicine (NLM) and the National Agriculture Library (NAL) are unquestionably influenced and heavily so by their respective clientele, namely the entrenched corporate hierarchies of the health-care juggernaut and global agri-business, that provide the funding for the research which ends up in the citation databases in the first place. A librarian wanting to assist a patron with a query on pesticide-free agriculture or homeopathy would be hard pressed to find much by way of an index or finding aid. There's simply no money in it, so it isn't produced in any meaningful manner, and neither of the above-mentioned citation databases is in any way comprehensive on these topics.

The point here is that there is nowhere a debate in the library press, and least of all at NAL or NLM, about the a priori assumptions that underpin the "well-meaning" creation of these databases, glossing over the fact that the dominant corporate paradigm of big health care and big agri-business are the dominant purveyors of the "information" indexed. There's a tacit acceptance that "that's just the way things are in the real world," so "what are we supposed to do?" As one librarian at NAL told this author when he asked about the inclusion of alternative agriculture systems in AGRICOLA: "We have been given strict guidelines about what is considered acceptable science and what isn't. Many of the journals covering organic topics are not refereed and therefore do not meet minimum criteria for inclusion." Needless to say, the thousands of items produced by state farm bureaus which AGRICOLA indexes annually are hardly science; in fact much of the Farm Bureau material is sponsored by big pesticide companies hawking their toxins. The point is unambiguous. Since the Farm Bureau represents mainstream agriculture par excellence and has big bucks behind it, it gets included. Organic agriculture, by comparison, tends to be local, marginalized, and cash poor, ergo it lacks the clout to self-organize and be heard. The library database AGRICOLA reflects this bias to its discredit. The basic tenets of this argument can be applied to dozens of other indexes and databases and there's the rub.

In a letter received by this author from Sanford Berman, Head Cataloger of the Hennepin County Library (HCL) in Minnesota, Mr. Berman wrote:

> More classism evidence. Although HCL has been suggesting new subject headings to LC [Library of Congress] for some 3 years now...., the following are still not established, meaning that the very topics/issues themselves don't appear in library catalogs and thus don't seem to be "real": CLASSISM, ENVIRONMENTAL RACISM, CORPORATE POWER, CORPORATE WELFARE.

Mr. Berman's observations are on target. Since the very usage of language in our culture is defined and expressed via centralized sources of distribution such as television and radio, or as in this case by LC subject headings, it becomes increasingly difficult to even frame the nature of the debate. The very words which define these interrelationships and avenues of power have been expunged from the public vocabulary by the purveyors of our common culture, e.g. big business and media conglomerates and by extension, by their lackies, state and federal government, of which LC is clearly, if unconsciously, a part.

The same story circulates throughout the profession, in special, public, and academic libraries, in our science and humanities collections respectively, and in our protocols of professional behavior across the board. That corporations dominate our profession as publishers, hardware manufacturers, software providers, database creators, and network gatekeepers, and that an attendant corporate ethic increasingly infuses how library management defines its modus operandi, is a sad fact we, as progressive librarians, must contend with. The hope that organizations such as the American Library Association, or even the Special Library Association, infused as it is with corporate membership, are likely to find their voice to call a halt to this hell-bent romance between corporate-dominated paradigms and the way libraries do their business, is farfetched and unlikely in the extreme.

As with any social cause, the call to action will doubtless come from rank and file members of the profession who are willing to loudly proclaim their outrage. Only through constant agitation is there some modicum of hope that the profession might possibly be awakened from its complacency, but it will be an uphill struggle every step of the way. For one, it is so terribly difficult to even open up the true terms of the debate without immediate ridicule by the champions of the status quo. And there will be fierce resistance as well. Our unquestioning fascination with technology and with the bottom lines of smart business practice, with the desire to streamline operations, and by our obvious acceptance of corporate-library partnerships, these are powerful forces indeed with entrenched and fiercely partisan protagonists.

Elements of this call to action to oppose corporate inroads in librarianship might reasonably be expected to enlist some of the following thirteen tactics:

Be skeptical about fiscal and other "crises"
Take economics seriously, learn the "facts"
Challenge hypocrisy
Maximize every obstacle
Work hard to maintain solidarity
Encourage concerned users to speak out
Establish coalitions with other librarians and other

libraries
Support those who speak out
Develop alternative media options
Resist market-speak
Be pro-active
Challenge the TINA ("there is no alternative") claim
Promote participatory democracy

This piece began with talk of choice. Librarianship is obviously at a crossroads. As we near the 21st century, we must ask ourselves what is it as librarians that we hold most dear. Is it a clear and unambiguous adherence to the First Amendment or is it to community standards of propriety? Is it to the inalienable provisions of a free and welcoming civic space open to every citizen in this harried world or is it to a shopping mall mentality hawking infotainment where the homeless, the poor and unwashed are unwelcome? Do we want big business running our business? And what about technology? As material content (books, journals, reference resources, print collections, etc.) migrate to electronic formats and are increasingly rendered useless in and of themselves without the electronic gadgetry and electricity which alone can access them (thus rendering as a single mechanism the content and the delivery medium), will our professional standing in our society become synonymous with hardware mechanics and CPU tinkerers? Are we ready for the unending push to upgrade our gadgetry and software every other year at exorbitant cost and at the undoubted expense of personally serving our users? To be sure, these are hard questions. But if we wish to adhere fiercely to the First Amendment, to preserve the open door policy of libraries as civic forums, if we are committed to shunning non-stop corporate huckstering at our very workstations, and to slowing the relentless march to digitization (in order to formulate and examine its implications at every step coherently, on our terms, not Microsoft's), then each and every one of us had better infuse into our daily practice a meaningful discussion of these issues and openly examine their implications among our colleagues, patrons, and administrators. Short of that, the Exxon Reading Room will be coming to a library near you!

(The author wishes to express special thanks to Sanford Berman, Charles Willet, and others on the PLG listserv who assisted him with this article. Thanks to Dr. Jane Kelsey of the University of New Zealand for the list of tactics.)

Works Cited

Baker, N. (1994) Annals of scholarship: Discards. *New Yorker, 70*(7), 64-86.

Buschman, J. (1994) Librarians, self-censorship, and information technologies. *College & Research Libraries*, 55, 221-8.

Carpenter, B. (1997, January 15). Re: Hawaii updates and the future plans of outsourcing. Message posted to PLGNet-L.

Chaffee, J. (1995, May). Commercializing the library. *The Independent* (San Francisco), p. 2.

Cullars, J. (1984) An analysis of reviews and library holdings of small publishers' books. *Library Resources and Technical Services, 28*, 4-14.

Denwall. (n.d.). Re: Demoralization among librarians in Hawaii. Message posted to PLGNet-L.

Lee, E. (1995). Small publishers and big libraries: How bureaucracy and hugeness work to suppress non-mainstream ideas. *Alternative Press Review,* (Winter), 12-13.

Mutter, J. (1988) Baker & Taylor targets the trade. *Publishers Weekly, 234*, (July 22), 34.

OCLC. (n.d.). History of OCLC. Retrieved from http://www.oclc.org/about/history/defaulthtm.

School Library Journal. (1996). *42*, (December), 38.

Serebnick, J. (1992). Selection and holdings of small publishers' books in OCLC libraries: A study of the influence of reviews, publishers and vendors. *The Library Quarterly, 62*, 259-295.

Tomioka, C. (1997, January 15) Re: Update on material sent to you. Posted to PLGNet-L.

West, C. (1983). The secret garden of censorship: Ourselves. *Library Journal*, 108, 1651-3.

[Note: "Corporate Inroads and Librarianship: The Fight for the Soul of the Profession in the New Millenium" originally appeared in *Progressive Librarian*, Nos. 12/13, Spring/Summer 1997.]

Librarianship and Resistance

By Sandy Iverson

In "The End of Innocence," Jane Flax (1992) concludes her essay by stating that "at its best, postmodernism invites us to engage in a continual process of disillusionment with the grandiose fantasies that have brought us to the brink of annihilation" (p. 460). To me, this is the hope of postmodernism and since reading Flax's article I have reflected on some of the particular "grandiose fantasies" or "metanarratives" that have structured my own life both personally and professionally.

I am trained as a librarian, and for a number of years I have focused my work in the "alternative" library sector. In this work I have been engaged in building and providing access to collections of resources not usually found in public, academic, or other mainstream libraries. Both in my training and in my work I have often felt ambivalent about librarianship and been at odds with the "library establishment." In reflecting on some of the metanarratives that underlay librarianship I begin to understand my own discomfort with the library establishment and with the practice of librarianship. I also begin to understand that I continue to accept unquestioningly too many of these metanarratives.

As our global society becomes increasingly based on the commodity of information, power becomes increasingly focused and managed by those with access to information. Those without such access remain marginalized. Librarians have been trained in the management of information. Therefore, I see their role as inherently political. Unfortunately, all too often librarians have rejected the political nature of the work they do. In these times of increased commodification of information, librarians have sought to play leading roles in the new "information society." In order to do so, they have uncritically accepted the ideals of professionalization and have embraced the principles of objectivity and neutrality.

William Birdsall (1982), a librarian at Dalhousie University, has examined this issue and he fears that by uncritically adopting the stance of objectivity librarians might too easily perceive their role to be at the service of the knowledge elites; indeed, they could too eagerly concentrate on trying to insure for themselves a place among these elites while losing sight of their obligation to serve a broad clientele (p.223).

Librarians tend to see themselves as neutral service providers, rejecting any stated political stance, and certainly their training encourages this position. As Henry Blanke (1989) maintains: "Librarianship's reluctance to define its values in political terms and to cultivate a sense of social responsibility may allow it to drift into an uncritical accommodation with society's dominant political and economic powers" (p.39).

While librarians are trained to maintain an objective or neutral stance they are also expected to make decisions regarding "good" and "bad" materials. Librarians are often seen as "experts" in determining the literature and other resources that their clientele needs. Unfortunately, they do not often recognize the inherent bias at work in making these decisions. Librarians generally regard the selection of materials as apolitical.

Donna Haraway (1991) has written a compelling critique of the "myth" of objectivity. She sees "objectivity doctrines [to be] in the service of hierarchical and positivist orderings of what can count as knowledge" (Haraway, p. 188). Certainly librarians have served these same "hierarchical and positivist" orders in determining the "knowledge" that will be made available to their public. Haraway calls for a new feminist understanding of objectivity: "I would like a doctrine of embodied objectivity that accommodates paradoxical and critical feminist science projects: feminist objectivity means quite simply situated knowledges" (p.188). Haraway explains that what we have accepted as "objectivity" claims to be a vision of the world from everywhere at once: "But of course that view of infinite vision is an illusion, a god trick" (p. 189). We can not see from all perspectives at once, we each have our own particular views that are shaped by our own identities, cultures, experiences, and locations. "Feminist objectivity is about limited location and situated knowledge..." (Haraway, p.190). I suggest that librarians could better serve the interests of all of their public by adopting Haraway's model and recognizing their own multiple, situated knowledges and those of their constituencies.

Connected to the "metanarrative" of objectivity within librarianship is the concept of intellectual freedom. Librarians have been vocal defenders of freedom of information and freedom of speech. In many cases, librarian's anti-censorship stance has been in reaction to their being lobbied to censor or ban certain materials. This stance has been directly related to their belief in their own objectivity. They believe in their responsibility to provide access to a wide variety of information.

However, as Philip (1990) points out, "the ideological framework of Western democracies has been erected upon and is supported as much by the ideology of freedom of the individual (and its offshoots) as by the ideology of racism. However, one discourse, censorship, becomes privileged; the other, racism, is silenced" (Philip, p. 210). While librarians have been avidly anti-censorship, they have not been avidly anti-racist. In fact, they do not acknowledge the inherent racism that is active within the discourse of anti-censorship.

Philip discusses the debates that have raged around the issue of white middle class writers writing from the point of view of those of differing class or racial backgrounds. In doing so, these writers make it even more difficult for writers of other cultures and races to become published as these groups have, by the "exploitive practices of capitalist economies ... [been deprived] of the ability to express themselves through writing and publishing" (Philip, 1990, p.213). Systemic racism in our society typically limits access to resources to all but the privileged white middle class; by doing so society effectively "censors" many voices. Consequently, librarians responsible for acquisitions may be recreating racist censorship in their daily practices of selecting from lists of materials produced by mainstream publishing houses and other organizations that perpetuate these patterns.

Additionally, librarians need to examine the practices of how they treat the materials that they do receive. For instance, David Lane, an American librarian, has examined the practice of libraries obtaining information on South Africa from the South African consulate. Consequently, he found that many libraries' pamphlet file collections neglected to include any information that was critical of apartheid. While it may be useful to include overtly racist materials in a library collection, the challenge for librarians is in how these materials are categorized and filed. Librarians must be challenged to treat racist materials as racist materials. Generally, libraries adopt standard classification schemes, such as the Library of Congress, which do not encourage such treatment. Therefore, we might often find hate propaganda classified as historical documents, or literature, rather than as hate literature. Similarly, librarians should challenge the standard resources that they use and supply to their public. Polly Thistlethwaite, an AIDS activist and librarian, examined the problem of exclusion of

AIDS information in periodical indexes. Thistlethwaite (1991) found that "gay/lesbian periodicals and community-based health publications containing vital, often vanguard HIV/AIDS information are systematically excluded from mainstream indexes and database services" (p. 35). Thistlethwaite maintains that how the decisions to ignore these materials are made "lie deeply embedded in Western politics and culture, reflected in our media, government, and religious institutions defining mainstream and alternative 'lifestyles,' normal from deviant sexual behavior, innocent from deserving people with AIDS" (Thistlethwaite, p. 35-36). In other words the exclusion of these materials from standard indexes and databases reflects the homophobia that is rampant in our society. Librarians, by their non-critical reliance on these standard sources perpetuate homophobic practices.

Free and universal access to information (like literacy and education) is often upheld as a major tenet of the democratic society. Ostensibly the Canadian system of public libraries was established on this fundamental belief. However, some would argue that the establishment of public libraries was not as connected to the professed good of the people, as it was established to counter popular movements and popular knowledge with the provision of established "good knowledge." In a study of township libraries in Canada West during the period 1846-1860, Bruce Curtis (1985) found that in establishing these libraries,

> even those eager to guard what they described as "our religious liberty" and "our civil and social right and natural interests" argued that well-regulated libraries were important because of the consequences of literacy upon "the favourable development of the individual character."... Many political glosses might be given to the concept of "popular intelligence," but library proponents commonly pointed to "the great importance of furnishing the working population of our country with food for the mind" as a crucial "means of raising them in the scale of moral intelligence." However much library proponents were convinced of the inherent "goodness" of public libraries, it is at least clear that libraries were conceived as alternatives to some cultural practices, and as politically potent institutions (p. 8).

It seems that the "cultural practices" that libraries were conceived as alternatives to, were primarily the habit of public house drinking and the types of discussion and literature that was shared during these evenings of camaraderie and drink. Great concern was expressed by the ruling class of the day as to the idleness and public house habits of the working class. Libraries were established, at least in part, to counteract these subversive activities.

Given these less than equitable and politically oppressive beginnings, it perhaps should not surprise us that many of the underlying concepts that govern the everyday work of librarianship continue to perpetuate systems of domination in our society. However, librarians continue to be educated and to progress in their careers with the belief that their role, while crucial to a democratic society, is not in the least political. The role of information in our society becomes increasingly central and as it does, many questions need to be raised. If we accept that information is connected to knowledge and knowledge to power, we must examine the connections between power and information in our postmodern society. What are the implications for increased access to information by the dominant segment of society? Librarians are trained in the expert manipulation of information by mastering the technology connected to the production, dissemination, and retrieval of information. However, what are the implications for society in not questioning what kinds of information are accessible and what kinds are not, and who has easy access?

While technology has increased access to information, at the same time we are experiencing funding cutbacks to the public library system. At the very time that universal access to information may be reachable, financial support by the state diminishes. This "coincidence" should not go unexamined. In order to continue service, libraries are beginning to charge user fees for certain services. This practice contradicts the tenet of equal access to information, and may eventually result in the extinction of the public library system. In order to continue to provide career opportunities for their students, many library schools have shifted their focus to train librarians for careers in the corporate (or private) library world. Less and less attention is paid to public or community library service. I would like to call on librarians, and librarian educators, to examine their practices in light of postmodern thought. We need to question our practices, and the underlying concepts that govern these practices. I grant that during this time of "emerging national and global structures of information-capitalism" (Jansen, 1989, p. 196) librarians do have a critical role to play. However, I would argue that their role should not be to act in "collusion with the forces which perpetuate disadvantage" (Harris, 1991, p.75), but to redefine their role to assist in the establishment of a truly equitable society. In order to do this I would urge librarians and librarian educators to begin to question the "metanarratives" that librarianship is built upon. I would urge us all to begin by following Donna Haraway's advice to adopt a position of situated knowledge and partial perspective. Adopting such a position is key to our learning to live together equitably. As Haraway pointed out:

> We do not seek partiality for its own sake, but for the sake of the connections and unexpected openings situated knowledge make possible. The only way to find a larger vision is to be somewhere in particular (1991, p. 197).

Specifically Haraway urges us to pay particular attention to those knowledges that have historically been marginalized: "Subjugated" standpoints are preferred because they seem to promise more adequate, sustained, objective, transforming accounts of the world" (p.191). Perhaps by following her advice, we can succeed in establishing a truly alternative library sector, one that can be instrumental in resisting the dominating influences "that have brought us to the brink of annihilation" (Flax, 1992, p. 460).

Works Cited

Birdsall, W.F. (1982). Librarianship, professionalism, and social change. *Library Journal, 107,* 223-226.

Blanke, H.T. (1989). Librarianship and political values: Neutrality or commitment? *Library Journal, 114,* 39-43.

Curtis, B. (1985). "Littery merritt", "useful knowledge" and the organization of township libraries in Canada West, 1846-60. Unpublished paper written at the Ontario Institute for Studies in Education, Toronto.

Flax, J. (1992). The end of innocence. In J. Butler & J. Scott (Eds.), *Feminists theorize the political.* Toronto: Routledge.

Haraway, D. (1991). *Simians, cyborgs, and women.* New York: Routledge.

Harris, K. (1991). Information and social change in the 1990s. *International Journal of Information and Library Research*, *3*(1): 75-85.

Jansen, S.C. (1989). Gender and the information society: A socially structured silence. *Journal of Communication*, *39*(3), 196-215.

Lane, D. (1990). Your pamphlet file supports apartheid. *Library Journal*, *115*, 174-177.

Philip, M.N. (1990). The disappearing debate. In L. Scheier, et al. (Eds.), *Language in her eye*. Toronto: Coach House.

Thistlethwaite, Polly. (1991). AIDS information in periodical indexes: A problem of exclusion. *Reference Services Review*, *19*(2), 35-38.

["Librarianship and resistance" originally appeared in *Progressive Librarian*, No. 15, Winter 1998/1999.]

A Few Gates Redux: An Examination of the Social Responsibilities Debate in the Early 1970s and 1990s

By Steven Joyce

Social responsibility will someday become once again a burning issue for libraries. Others will come together with new hope, new Congresses for Change, new challenges to make the tired and sterile professional mind whirl about in confusion and anger (Armitage, 1973, p. 41).

He who defines the terms wins the argument (Josey, 1973, p. 32).

Introduction
1992

The July/August 1992 cover photo of *American Libraries* (*AL*) depicts a nondescript group of people standing behind a banner that reads: "Gay and Lesbian Task Force: American Library Association" (Appendix I). The reaction to the cover by *AL* readership was swift, virulent, and homophobic:

> I was very displeased by the front cover displaying gay and lesbian librarians marching down Market Street. . . as a matter of fact I wanted to *puke!* I have already been called on the carpet by library board members who feel the American Library Association [ALA] is a "lunatic fringe" association [emphasis in original]. (Witt, 1992, p. 625)

> I still find it reprehensible that an association I am a member of chooses to glorify homosexuals. The vast majority of the American people do not support such a lifestyle that flies in the face of sound family values and a healthy physical and mental well-being. (Hartwell, 1992, p. 843)

> When I saw how ALA is not a professional organization, but a left wing political group, I vowed that it would never receive a penny from me again. . . . We think homosexuality is WRONG—W-R-O-

N-G. It is against God's laws. . . . I propose that all God-fearing librarians start up an alternative library organization [emphasis in original]. (Michell, 1992, p. 843).

AL editor Tom Gaughan pointed out that

> ...just 24 hours after the advance copies. . . of *AL* reached our offices, I began to get educated by readers who were irate over the cover photo.
>
> The first call was from a man so livid he had difficulty speaking. . . he "didn't care what people do behind closed doors" but it didn't belong on the cover of his professional association's magazine. He also said he "lived in a nice neighborhood" and didn't want anyone to see something like *AL*'s cover in his mailbox...I was startled at the depth of the fear and anger in his voice...What are they seeing on the cover, I wondered—a group of people standing behind a banner, or sex acts? The second caller made an analogy between gays and murderers...Several callers criticized the "very poor taste" and the "very poor editorial decision" of selecting the offending cover photo...Another complained that as a school librarian she didn't want her students to see it...The fear and loathing apparent in their voices was more eloquent than their words. (1992, p. 612)

Intermixed with the more extreme reactions were the calm and reasoned if somewhat patronizing arguments against the advocacy of non-library social issues apparently elicted by the cover photo.

> I'm probably as firm an advocate of Afro-American—Native-American—gay and lesbian rights as anyone, but I'd like to see the library profession cease its endless advocacy of social issues and return to the difficult issues of operating information agencies. (Brace, 1992, p. 738)

> When an organization espouses extreme views it runs a strong risk of losing credibility and effectiveness in its primary function. The question is not whether gays and lesbians are discriminated against, but whether this is an appropriate or relevant issue for ALA. (Rasimus, 1992, p. 625).

Whether *AL*'s cover photo advocated "extreme views" on issues irrelevant to librarianship is debatable, but it did have the effect of polarizing various factions within the library community.

According to one view, which allies itself primarily with ALA's Library Bill of Rights (Appendix II), ALA involvement with social issues must be limited and directly related to librarianship (Uricchio, 1994). The arguments for this view are fairly simple and straightforward. Librarians must remain neutral with respect to social issues outside the purview of librarianship, and they must focus only on the provision of equitable access to as many points of view as possible. Further, in a climate of reduced budgets and increased work loads, librarians have more than enough work in terms of fulfilling basic institutional goals and objectives without spending time and resources on causes that only marginally involve the profession.

Another view, not necessarily antithetical to the Library Bill of Rights, has it that social issues outside the purview of librarianship must be investigated. The arguments in favor of this view tend to be somewhat more complex than those for the neutralist position. Buschman, Rosenzweig, and Harger (1994) argue that "calls for ALA to purge social issues from its substantial and varied agenda are unhealthy for the profession, destructive of internal democracy, fundamentally hypocritical, and intellectually unsound" (p. 575). They argue this for several reasons. First, librarians must become actively engaged in the society they serve. Librarianship concerns itself with literacy, intellectual freedom, and equity of information access. By holding such values, they ask, how can librarians ignore issues concerning basic human dignity and the social conditions in which human culture develops? Second, rather than eliminating debate on social issues, such debate should be seen as a sign of a healthy intellectual community. Third, who is to decide what is and is not of primary concern to librarianship? Not every political and social issue relates to the library profession, but it is the job of ALA's Social Responsibilities Round Table (SRRT) to raise such issues so that their implications for librarianship can be discussed (Buschman et al., p. 576). Indeed, in areas where librarians can lose their jobs on the basis of a nonconforming sexual orientation, gay rights, as both a political and social issue, becomes directly relevant within the context of librarianship. Thus, it is both unrealistic and naïve to think that librarians and librarianship can be divorced from the political and social realities within which they operate.

This ongoing debate focusing on social responsibilities is not particularly new, and many of the arguments employed today, both for and against, were employed well over 25 years ago. In fact, *AL*'s cover photo became the catalyst through which the largely dormant social responsibilities debate of the late 1960s and early 1970s was reawakened and re-cast. Should ALA or, for that matter, any professional library association advocate on behalf of social issues not directly relevant to the practice of librarianship? What about individual librarians? Should they advocate on behalf of social issues not directly relevant to the practice of librarianship? Would not such advocacy be tantamount to catering to special interest groups and, as such, detract from the ideal of the balanced collection and the need to provide information to as many people as possible from as many points of view as possible? In the final analysis, would not such advocacy, whether by a professional association or by an individual librarian, detract from equitable access to materials and information for all? These questions can be examined in light of present day social attitudes toward those who, for many, constitute "the last socially acceptable prejudice" (Gaughan, 1992, p.612), those who reignited the social responsibilities debate within librarianship: gays, lesbians, and bisexuals. However, these questions should first be examined in light of the events that gave them birth from the founding of the SRRT in 1968 to the infamous Berninghausen debate of the early 1970s.

1967-1971

Boris Raymond (1979) has pointed out that prior to 1968, an old guard of established library administrators dominated ALA and kept the association's activities tightly focused on the promotion of library institutions (p. 349). In fact, even as late as the 1967 ALA Conference, nary a whisper was heard in protest against an entrenched old-guard leadership and its narrowly focused agenda. However, initial rumblings began only a few months later when Harold Taylor, speaking at the Middle Atlantic Regional Library Conference of October 1967, warned:

> Until recently we have not been conscious of the fact that the world revolution has its counterpart in the social revolution now happening in our own country, where the underclass. . . are demanding that their rights be recognized in such a way that they too can enjoy the privileges shared by the American middle class. If they are not fulfilled by intelligent, compassionate, and cooperative social action involving   all of society . . . they will be achieved by force and violence. (1968, p. 510)

Indeed, the next year saw immense social upheaval characterized by civil and racial unrest, political rioting, student uprisings, and resistance to the Vietnam War. Much of the West's cultural ideology underwent a shift to the left, a shift that took with it the fertile minds of young librarians and newly graduated library students. And so, at the June 1968 ALA Conference in Kansas City, business was not quite as usual. At the membership meeting, a number of resolutions were introduced, most notable of which was Kenneth Duchac's "motion calling for the establishment of a Round Table on the Social Responsibility of Libraries" ("Business," 1968, p. 2797). Duchac spoke eloquently and passionately with, perhaps, a hint of hyperbole, on behalf of a coalition of younger librarians, recent library graduates, and various politically marginalized groups (including "black militants, political radicals, members of women's liberation groups, and individuals interested in library unions" [Raymond, 1979, p. 354]) who wished to dilute the ranks of the conservative ALA leadership and divest it of some of its control:

> One need not have the wisdom of Solomon to know that the events of this year, unprecedented in our history, are indices of a force of change which is accelerating at such a colossal rate and with such a burning intensity that we as a people and a nation are in a condition where intransigence is replacing flexibility, and where extremes of action—of anarchy or fascism—are possible, even probable, for the first time in over 100 years.
>
> It was the request of our petition that ALA provide an outlet for expression of libraries' and librarians' concerns on these issues—race, violence, war and peace, inequality of justice and opportunity—by creating a Round Table on the Social Responsibilities of Libraries. ("Business," 1968, p. 2799)

Duchac's plea aroused much interest, and, after intense and animated discussion (with little actual debate), the motion passed easily. However, it still needed Council's approval.

Following required protocol, ALA's Membership Committee called upon the Committee on Organization (COO) to recommend the motion to ALA Council for approval by the end of the week. Such a tight deadline, while imposed by a fervored Membership Committee, seemed ridiculously short for many who felt the need to examine and consider fully the implications of creating a Social Responsibilities Round Table. Nevertheless, because of the motion's perceived urgency by round table advocates, Council was recalled immediately after the membership meeting. Quorum, however, was not achieved, and President Foster Mohrhardt called a special Council meeting for the following day. At that meeting COO Chair Robert Sheridan attempted to underplay the urgency of the proposed round table and, to some extent, undermine Duchac's motion. After prolonged and often acrimonious debate, council member Father Jovian Lang warned: "Yesterday's was a controlled and sensible revolution. But if we do not give serious consideration to the members' urgency, yesterday's events will be nothing compared to what is to come" ("Business," 1968, p. 2800). Council opted to ignore the good Father's advice and voted to remove the deadline imposed on COO by the Membership Committee. And yet, due to rapidly growing pressure within the ALA membership, COO did ultimately recommend the motion, and Council did approve it by the end of the week. At the end of June 1968, the Social Responsibilities Round Table met unofficially for the first time, its mandate later defined:

1. To provide a forum for the discussion of the responsibilities of libraries in relation to the important problems of social change which face institutions and librarians;
2. To provide for exchange of information among all ALA units about library activities with the goal of increasing understanding of current social problems;
3. To act as a stimulus to the Association and its various units in making libraries more responsive to current social needs;
4. To present programs, arrange exhibits and carry out other appropriate activities. (ALA, Social Responsibilities Round Table 1970, cited from Stevens, 1989, p. 18).

Almost a year later, in late March 1969, a group of University of Maryland library students gathered for a two day session to discuss changes in library education ("ALAiad," 1969, p. 80). Broader issues were also discussed including an ALA leadership which was unresponsive to its members' needs, ALA election reform, and grass-roots support of intellectual freedom; and, it was decided that a larger conference would be held in June immediately preceding ALA's Atlantic City Conference. Thus was born the Congress for Change (CFC).

On June 19, 1969, CFC members descended on the Manger-Annapolis Hotel in Washington, DC for what would be the first and, in effect, last full CFC conference (Nelson, 1987, p. 127). "[A]bout 100 young and youngish people dedicated to smashing the status quo" ("ALAiad," 1969, p. 80) met to develop a program of action. The attending delegates had no interest in listening to platitudinous speeches, however well intentioned. They came to express their views and to seek support for those views. According to John Berry, *Library Journal (LJ)* editor, "a more impressive gathering of U.S. librarians we have not experienced. Impressive not because of its power or stature, but because, for the first time in our experience there was a single-minded attack on the age-old problems of the profession and the library institution" (1969, p. 2727). Despite Berry's enthusiasm, this "nonconference" was, as one can well imagine, characterized by a lack of both structure and clearly articulated goals. While the focus in March had been primarily on library education, the focus in June had gravitated towards "whether or not the profession itself—particularly the American Library Association should be an instrument to basic change in American social and political policy" (Nelson, 1987, p. 127).

Shortly after, at the ALA Conference in Atlantic City, the CFC allied itself with the fledgling SRRT whose members opened up formal and informal channels for CFC members. In this way, the CFC could make its many and varied issues known to the greater library community. Faint rumblings of discontent emerged in the first hours of the conference, but it was not until the membership meeting convened that the first eruptions took place. The first speaker for the Congress spoke openly "of ALA's 'irrelevance' and 'inflexibility' [and] added that if changes were not made . . . the Congress for Change would be prepared 'to launch an active campaign to discourage membership in ALA'" ("ALAiad," 1969, p. 86). Resolution after resolution was proposed in what was to become one of the longest membership meetings in ALA conference history. "There were statements on intellectual freedom, accrediting library schools, military issues, poverty, advocacy, and activism" (Nelson, 1987, p. 129).

In the face of pressure from both the SRRT and the CFC, President William Dix announced the immediate establishment of the Activities Committee on New Directions (ACONDA—informally known as the Dix Mix) to re-examine the structure and goals of ALA and to make recommendations based on its findings. "Clearly, the SRRT and Congress for Change became a continuously vocal force and were in part assimilated into the ALA power structure" (Geller, 1969, p. 3136). One of the major issues that ACONDA faced was whether

ALA should become involved with questions of general social responsibility or whether it should focus only on issues directly affecting librarianship (Raymond, 1979, p. 356). Within a couple of months, ACONDA made recommendations on six critical issues:

- Social responsibilities
- Manpower
- Intellectual freedom
- Legislation
- Planning, research, and development
- Democratization and reorganization ("ACONDA summary," 1970, p. 685).

During a marathon sixteen hour membership meeting at the 1970 ALA Conference in Detroit, ACONDA's recommendations were examined, discussed, and voted on. Here, ACONDA officially defined the broad social responsibilities of ALA in terms of:

(a) the contribution that librarianship can make in ameliorating or even solving the critical problems of society, (b) support for all efforts to help inform and educate the people of the United States on these problems and to encourage them to examine the many views on, and the facts regarding, each problem, and (c) the willingness of ALA to take a position on current critical issues, with the relationship to libraries and library service clearly set forth in this position statement ("New directions," 1970, p. 938)

However, during the meeting, ALA Treasurer Bob McClarren warned that acceptance of social responsibilities outside the purview of librarianship could result in a loss of ALA's favored tax-exempt status (Berry, 1970, p. 2615). After much debate and political maneuvering, the membership accepted most of the Committee's proposed recommendations and sent them to Council. Council adopted the recommendations that constituted statements of principle, but it deferred recommendations that required some form of implementation including the section on social responsibilities. In order to further study these recommendations, Council devised its own Ad Hoc Committee on ACONDA (ANACONDA) which made further recommendations on five of the six critical issues mentioned above ("Recommendations," 1971). Perhaps McClarren's warning of a loss of tax-exempt status struck fear into the hearts of ANACONDA members, because the issue of social responsibilities vanished altogether from the agenda.

To be fair, ACONDA and ANACONDA did take concrete action on several important issues. For instance, they took an official stand against discrimination towards gays and lesbians within libraries, they set up a manpower office to work on behalf of the welfare of librarians, and they set up the Committee on Mediation, Arbitration, and Inquiry (Raymond, 1979, p. 358). However, despite these advances, ALA had been able to neatly side-step the SRRT's essential although controversial and contentious issue of social responsibilities (Samek, 1996, p. 57).

1972-1973

Many within the ALA power structure felt that the concept of social responsibilities was antithetical to the principles embodied within the Library Bill of Rights, and that acceptance of one would, by definition, negate acceptance of the other. Perhaps the loudest proponent of this antithesis, and the one whose voice still echoes through the library literature of today, was David K. Berninghausen, director of the now defunct University of Minnesota Library School. Berninghausen had also occupied the chair of ALA's Intellectual Freedom Committee (IFC) from 1948 to 1952 and again from 1967 to 1972. During the early 1970s, he published a series of articles, which culminated in a book entitled *The flight from reason* (1975). Through these writings, he expressed his opposition to the newly developed concept of social responsibilities

In "The librarian's commitment to the Library Bill of Rights" (1970), Berninghausen examined the history of both the Library Bill of Rights and the IFC from their inception in 1939 and 1940 respectively through to the late 1960s. With an eye to the future, he warned librarians to be cautious of those on the radical left and the reactionary right, those who were prepared to further their causes by any possible means:

> Probably no group, under or over thirty, black or white, religious or anti-religious, of the political left or the political right, is without a few members who are so extreme, so rigid, so intransigent that they sincerely believe that anyone who does not view the world precisely as they do should be forced to conform or cease to exist (1970, p. 35).

He then immediately pointed out that ACONDA's "re-definition" of social responsibilities rejected the "traditional, conservative" definition—a definition which he never fully articulated, but which, one can safely assume, focused on librarian neutrality—and he followed up by citing at length the first report of ACONDA's Subcommittee on Social Responsibility:

> Social Responsibility is considered radical, new, activist. It can best be summed up by a definition put forth by ALA's Committee on Organization: "Social responsibilities can be defined as the relationships that librarians and libraries have to non-library problems that relate to the social welfare of our society" (American Library Association, 1970, p. 2; as cited in Berninghausen, 1970, p. 36).

Did intransigent extremists, in an effort to hijack ALA and eradicate the Library Bill of Rights, redefine the traditional concept of social responsibilities (whatever that might be) and turn it into a radical, new, and activist (negative terms in Berninghausen's parlance) endeavor? Perhaps not, but through the structure of his prose, Berninghausen created a direct link between extremism and the concept of social responsibility; and, based on his interpretation of the definition of a subcommittee, the tired old neutralist stance as apparently espoused by the Library Bill of Rights was no longer viable. In his view, librarians were now being encouraged, by subversive forces within ALA, to embrace a new form of advocacy or partisan librarianship. In short, Berninghausen set up an implicit syllogism:

1. Those who hold intensely dogmatic beliefs are censorial;
2. Advocates of the new definition of social responsibility hold intensely dogmatic beliefs;
3. Advocates of the new definition of social responsibility are censorial and must, therefore, renounce the tenets of intellectual freedom.

For Berninghausen, the newly defined concept of social responsibility was antithetical to the principles of intellectual freedom, and it is with this view that he was to proceed in his further writings.

Berninghausen's *tour de force* arrived after the SRRT and CFC furor had begun to die down. In the November 1972 issue of *LJ*, he published "Social responsibility vs. the Library Bill of Rights," which was immediately followed up by nineteen rejoinders gathered together as

"The Berninghausen debate" in January 1973 (Wedgeworth *et al*). Berninghausen advanced his first major premise by stating that the *raison d'être* of ALA is, among other things, *not* any of the following:

1. To eradicate racial injustice and inequities and to promote human brotherhood.
2. To stop the pollution of air, earth, and sea.
3. To build a United Nations capable of preventing all wars (1972, p. 3675).

"Vital as these issues are, *it is not the purpose of ALA to take positions as to how men* [sic] *must resolve them* [emphasis in original]" (p. 3675). Interestingly, Berninghausen failed to explain the actual purpose of ALA, and, given the nature of the debate, the purpose of ALA did *not* go without saying. Further, Berninghausen's assertion begged the question: if it were not the purpose of ALA to take a stand on social issues such as those mentioned above, then just whose purpose was it? As Betty-Carol Sellen, one of the rejoinder authors, explained: "If librarians decide that the issues vital to society are irrelevant to librarians as librarians, then society may find that librarians are irrelevant to it" (Wedgeworth et al., 1973, p. 27).

Berninghausen went on to point out that it was not the purpose of ALA "to promote homosexualism as a life-style" (1972, p. 3675). Such a statement, noted Sellen, showed perfectly Berninghausen's inability to understand a socially responsible activity and its relevance to librarianship (Wedgeworth et al., 1973, p.27). The Gay Liberation Task Force of SRRT was formed in 1970 in order to help improve services to homosexuals and to help improve access to homosexual resources. At the time of Berninghausen's writing, homosexuals received little or no library service, libraries did not generally collect homosexual literature unless the content was clinical or disapproving (cf. Gittings, 1990), and Library of Congress Subject Headings were insulting and couched between other rather more unsavory headings (Greenblatt, 1990). Homosexuality was in fact listed as a sexual perversion and was linked to masochism, bestiality, and pederasty (Schrader, 1997, p. 150). Barbara Gittings, who chaired the Gay Liberation Task Force during its first 16 years, recalls:

> Today when I speak to gay groups and mention "the lies in the libraries," listeners over 35 know instantly what I mean. Most gays

have at some point gone to books in an effort to understand about being gay or to get some help in living as gay. In my time, what we found was strange to us (they're writing about me but I'm not like that!) and cruelly clinical (there's nothing about *love*) and always bad (being this way seems grim and hopeless) [emphasis in original] (1990, p. 2).

The real issue then was not the promotion of a life-style, as Berninghausen would have it, but rather a lack of access to useful and relevant resources for a politically and socially marginalized population. He implicitly raised an issue of which, at worst he was willfully ignorant, and at best he simply misunderstood; an issue which was, in fact, directly relevant to librarianship. Indeed, in his later book, *The flight from reason* (1975), one will note the irony in Berninghausen's statement that "the objective of strengthening library services to the disadvantaged is clearly a responsibility of libraries, librarians, and the ALA" (p. 111).

After leaving one with an arguably inaccurate and somewhat biased perception of the concept of social responsibilities, and after evading the issue that he himself raised (defining what actually is of relevance to librarianship), Berninghausen advanced his second major premise: if ALA becomes "a political and social organization, then the principle of intellectual freedom as stated in the Library Bill of Rights will have to be discarded" (1972, p. 3676). He provided no solid evidence for such a premise except through a series of imaginative anecdotes based on the implicit syllogism developed above. For example, in the early 1960s, Rachel Carson's *Silent spring* took aim at the pesticide DDT and claimed it to be a dangerous if not deadly chemical to both wildlife and human beings. For at least the next ten years, the book remained controversial in terms of its scientific validity. According to Berninghausen, librarians operating under the new social responsibility concept who agreed with Carson's analysis would insist that ALA take a stand on DDT, and they would provide "'guidance' on whether to ban *Silent spring* or criticisms of it." Why? Because those librarians "hold strong convictions, [and] hence must be right" (1972, p. 3678). Thus, not only would the very tenets of intellectual freedom be cast aside, ALA itself would be fractured from within on an issue unrelated to librarianship. If there were any doubt about Berninghausen's position, he made it crystal clear in *The flight from reason* (1975). In a fit of sarcasm, Berninghausen claimed that the proponents of social responsibility believed that

1. ALA should be politicized; that is, it should give up its professional character and its "traditional, conservative neutrality," becoming instead a partisan, advocacy organization.
2. Libraries should similarly be politicized. They should reject the Library Bill of Rights' concept of the library's professional responsibility to provide information on all sides of all controversial issues for all citizens. And publicly supported libraries should become "libraries of opinion" (1975, p. 109).

Just as Berninghausen "spun" the definition of social responsibilities as presented by the Subcommittee on Social Responsibility of ACONDA (1970), so too would he later make use of the same definition in order to inadvertently (one would hope) mislead the reader (Wedgeworth et al., 1973, p. 38). He first cited the subcommittee: "'[ALA] should endeavor to devise means whereby libraries can become more *effective instruments* to effect social change [emphasis mine]'" (1972, pp. 3676-7). (In fact, this statement comes not from the Subcommittee report, but from the ACONDA final report [Wedgeworth et al., 1973, p. 38]). He then rephrased the subcommittee's statement: "ALA and libraries. . . should be used as '*instruments to effect* social change [emphasis mine]'" (p. 3678). The difference between the two statements is not merely semantic. The first implies that libraries and librarians will enable users to effect social change; the second implies that libraries and librarians themselves will effect social change. Berninghausen changed the context of the original phrasing, and he carried the new context to his logical conclusion:

1. Librarians will become immersed in partisan causes unrelated to librarianship;
2. Librarians will reject the principle of intellectual freedom;
3. Librarians will censor materials with which they do not agree; and
4. Librarians will thereby attempt to effect social change based on their own dogmatic beliefs.

Ironically, Berninghausen never examined the stated purposes of the SRRT. It was doubly ironic that, while he warned librarians away from social issues, he did not explain how to avoid them. It was triply ironic that he appeared to break his own rule of misrepresentation: "it is only too common practice . . . to quote a limited passage out of context to produce a misleading picture" (1972, p. 3681).

1948

In order to better understand the context in which Berninghausen operated, it will prove fruitful to examine the path that was laid out for him. With the onset of the Cold War shortly after the end of World War II, the political climate in the United States underwent a drastic change. Americans embraced a unique pluralistic democracy that flatly rejected a fascistic or communistic totalitarianism. A reworked capitalist free enterprise system was characterized by the growth of diverse special interest groups and "free" thinkers along with an improved market economy. Paradoxically, because of the fear of communism, a challenge to the status quo could mean a challenge to the American way of life. By 1948, the House Un-American Committee had attacked the *Building America series* for its examination American's underbelly (slums, discrimination, moral decadence, etc.), and it was conducting hearings into the communist influence in the Hollywood film industry (Robbins, 1996, p. 30). The *Nation* had been banned in all New York City schools because of "a series of articles [deemed] disrespectful of the Catholic Church" (p. 32), and the "subversive" *New Republic* had been removed from the Champaign, IL public library. "In brief, that was the situation in June 1948. Was censorship a mountain or a molehill? The [Intellectual Freedom] Committee was not sure" (Berninghausen, 1953, p. 815).

The IFC, which was chaired by Berninghausen at the time, asked ALA to reaffirm the Library Bill of Rights (see Appendix III for the original Bill of 1939); and, at the Atlantic City conference of June 1948, the Bill underwent its first major revision (Appendix IV). A new article 3 introduced the need for librarians to challenge "censorship of books, urged or practiced by volunteer arbiters of morals or political opinion or by organizations that would establish a coercive concept of Americanism" (Appendix IV). This was the first time that censorship became an issue for the IFC, and it was the first time that the Library Bill of Rights explicitly called for libraries to challenge censorship. Also incorporated was a new article 4, which recognized the librarian's responsibility to cooperate with "allied groups. . . in science, education, and book publishing in resisting all abridgment of the free access to ideas and full freedom of expression" (Appendix IV). Indeed, as a result of the challenges of the 1950s, the newly revised Bill "moved from a little-known abstraction to a frequently invoked credo" (Robbins, 1996, p. 32).

While ALA unanimously passed the strengthened Library Bill of Rights, the resolution protesting loyalty investigations in libraries put forward at the same meeting ran into trouble. The intent of the resolution, which was sponsored by both the IFC and the Board on Personnel Administration, was to allow librarians to provide information on all points of view on controversial issues without fear of dismissal (Robbins, 1994, p. 366). The resolution did not have unanimous support as a number of federal librarians believed that filling out loyalty oaths would not compromise the tenets of intellectual freedom (p. 366). And despite the fact that the resolution passed, albeit narrowly, Librarian of Congress Luther Evans decreed: "'we don't want any Communists or cocksuckers in this library'" (cited in Robbins, 1994, p. 367). Henceforth, librarians thought to be gay or Communist were purged from the Library of Congress, and within a few years libraries throughout the country required loyalty oaths for continued employment (Carmichael, 1998).

Another aspect of post-war thinking incorporated the influence of scientific objectivity. Society began to rely increasingly on experts from such diverse fields as home economics, psychology, and urban planning; and these experts, in order to be seen as authoritative and professional, embraced the concept of scientific objectivity. Journalism emphasized facts, authority, and "hard" information; literary theory "killed" the author and looked only to the text; and art dispensed with all of its referents (Robbins, 1996, p. 31). At a time when commitment to a cause or the application of value could be seen as some form of communist plot and could arouse unwanted and potentially damning scrutiny, many professionals adopted some form of objectivity for protection. As a result, "librarians' insistence on 'objectivity' —their selection of books on all sides of controversial issues. . . even if they disagreed with the contents of the book—was intended both to elevate their standing as professionals and to protect their. . . jurisdiction of book selection from charges of bias" (p. 31). Throughout the McCarthy Era, Berninghausen saw a serious threat to intellectual freedom in terms of censorship and "objective" book selection from the far right. He perceived the same threat from the New Left in the late 1960s.

1967

The year 1967 saw another major revision to the Library Bill of Rights (Appendix V). A number of minor amendments were made, but the major changes focused on the particularly troublesome article 2 from 1948: "books or other reading matter of sound factual authority should not be proscribed or removed from library shelves because of partisan or doctrinal disapproval" (Appendix IV). The phrase "sound factual authority" could, in theory, allow librarians to use the Bill of Rights as a justification to proscribe or remove materials from library shelves. In the mid 1960s, this phrase was in fact used by a Catholic librarian in Belleville, IL to justify removal of a Protestant document from the library shelf (Office for Intellectual Freedom [OIF], 1992, p.9). The Belleville situation foregrounded the need for change, and at the 1967 ALA Conference, Council adopted the recommendations of the IFC: the phrase "books. . . of sound factual authority" was changed to read simply "library materials" (p. 11).

While both Berninghausen and the SRRT heralded the amendments, they interpreted the Bill in very different ways (for an excellent discussion of how one is to interpret the Library Bill of Rights, see *Library Trends* [1996] 45[1]). Berninghausen wished to preserve the status quo, and the new changes bolstered his concept of intellectual freedom in terms of maintaining a neutralist position. Librarians, in the performance of their duties, must collect materials on all sides of an issue but must never take sides. The SRRT, on the other hand, had its own conception of intellectual freedom. The Bill stated that libraries should provide materials "concerning problems and issues of our times" (OIF, 1992, p.11). From this, the Bill would seem to imply that librarians had a role to play in terms of those "problems and issues;" a role that implied more than mere collection development. Further, because the balanced collection was seen to be the ideal, the Bill seemed to imply that imbalanced collections should be actively redressed. For the SRRT, the newly amended Bill was a call to active participation for positive social change; for Berninghausen, it was the reinforcement of a neutrality that, in effect, maintained the status quo.

1974-1992

This brings us back to the events of the late 1960s and early 1970s. While the SRRT essentially deconstructed the universal claim of librarian neutrality, ALA had to deal with the sticky problem of its favored tax exempt status alluded to above. By 1974, the Internal Revenue Service was concerned about "certain activities" undertaken by "certain units" of ALA. Whether or not the profession agreed with the SRRT, "fear of social, financial, and legal repercussions . . . paralyzed the library community from further movement toward nonlibrary issues. . . . ALA membership was arguably less interested in the utility of the Library Bill of Rights than its own professional viability" (Samek, 1996, p. 59). Berninghausen and his ilk had won the day, and the status quo prevailed.

However, while ALA may have been under financial and legal constraints, individual librarians were not, and many adopted, if not the direct tenets, at least the spirit of the SRRT. Journal articles and entire books advocating general social responsibilities and calling for librarians to look beyond their library doors began to appear (see, for example, Jordan, 1975; Schuman, 1976; Martin, 1980; MacCann, 1989; and Stevens, 1989). Metta Winter (1983) advocated nuclear disarmament, and Carole Leita (1983) spent two weeks in jail for blocking the road to a nuclear laboratory. Roma Harris (1988) examined the information needs of battered women, and Elfreda Chatman entered the world of the low-income working-poor (1985a, 1985b, 1987a, 1987b), Cal Gough and Ellen Greenblatt (1990) focused on library services provided to gays and lesbians, and Ruth Velleman (1979) discussed the needs of the physically disabled. Sanford Berman (1981) has spent years railing against the inadequacies of Library of Congress Subject Headings; and, in 1989, the SRRT itself took an official stand against South African apartheid ("Guidelines"). Certainly none of these authors or organizations could be seen as neutral, and many of them focused on issues that only marginally, if at all, related to librarianship in a Berninghausian sense.

In 1984, Sanford Berman and James P. Danky launched *Alternative library literature: A biennial anthology*. The editors came to

> realize over the past decade that there's a wealth of variously wild, useful, dynamic, funny, provocative, and socially conscious "library literature" that few of our colleagues normally see. And that doesn't

make it into Katz's yearly anthology, which deliberately attempts to be "balanced." So here's the first volume ... a biennial, deliberately unbalanced collection of material dealing with library and information issues from a critical, nontraditional, socially responsible perspective; addressing topics usually overlooked or minimized in standard library media (p. 1).

As it turned out, many of the articles published in the anthology had previously been published in mainstream library literature including the likes of *Library Journal* and *Special Libraries*. For many, social issues and library issues became inextricably bound as librarians attempted to redress the injustices imposed by the status quo.

While the concept of social responsibilities appeared to be implicitly, if not explicitly, accepted by numerous librarians throughout the 1970s and 1980s, the principle of neutrality nonetheless dominated and remained the approved if largely unspoken standard. However, it was spoken loudly when *AL* published its cover photo in 1992.

The late 1960s were heady times and conspicuous for the activism they spawned. And it must be admitted that some of the New Left were in fact busy burning books, destroying card catalogues, and forcibly taking control of various institutions. The most extreme of these groups did attack the tenets of intellectual freedom, and it is unfortunate that Berninghausen and others made the error of assuming that any librarian who advocated the concept of social responsibilities was an extremist in her or his views.

So, why would a rather innocuous *AL* cover photo elicit such extreme reactions? Perhaps this can best be understood by a brief consideration of the early 1990s *zeitgeist*. By the early 1990s, discourse on homosexuality saturated the public æther more so than it had ever done since the Stonewall Uprising of 1969. (On June 28, 1969, New York City Police raided a gay bar called Stonewall Inn, which sparked three days of protest and rioting. For the first time, homosexuals fought back against the establishment, and the event has come to signify one of the most important landmarks in the struggle for gay rights.) Vice President Dan Quayle felt that homosexuality was not only a choice, but a wrong choice ("Malice," 1993, p. 4). President George H.W. Bush stated that, in his view, homosexuality was neither normal nor right (p. 4). On November 3, 1992, Colorado's Amendment Two, which prohibited municipalities from passing ordinances to protect the rights of lesbians and gays, went into effect (it was repealed by the Supreme Court in 1996). Ironically, ALA's 1992 Midwinter Meeting was held in Denver and this choice of location caused a great deal of controversy within the ALA rank and file. Many conferees marched on the Denver capital to protest the passage of the amendment (Berry et al., 1993, p. 35). Further, ALA President Marilyn Miller was the first and only ALA president to champion "the rights of lesbigay citizens both within and [notably] without the profession" (Carmichael, 1997, p. 13). In 1993, newly elected U.S. President Bill Clinton nominated Roberta Achtenberg, a lesbian, to the post of Assistant Secretary in the Department of Housing and Urban Development—the highest post ever offered to an openly homosexual person ("Clearances," 1992, p. 4). Clinton also instituted the disastrous "don't ask, don't tell" policy for homosexuals serving in the U.S. Armed Forces. As well, Paul Monette's memoir, *Becoming a man*, won a National Book Award; Tony Kushner's play, *Angels in America*, won a Pulitzer Prize; and, Tom Hanks portrayed a gay lawyer with AIDS in the film *Philadelphia*, for which he earned an Oscar for Best Actor. Finally, throughout the early 1990s, the FBI and the CIA were implicated in anti-homosexual hiring practices, new scientific evidence suggested that homosexuality might be the result of genetics, and right-wing fundamentalism was rapidly becoming media savvy in its fight against homosexuality. Indeed, by 1993, the "gay moment" had arrived:

> The gay moment is unavoidable. It fills the media, changes politics, saturates popular and elite culture. It is the stuff of everyday conversation and public discourse. Not for thirty years has a class of Americans endured the peculiar pain and exhilaration of having their civil rights and moral worth—their very humanness—debated at every level of public life (Kopkind, 1993, cover).

No longer relegated to the margins, the issue of homosexuality took center stage within the public domain for the first time *ever*. However, because of its focus on sexuality, itself socially and culturally problematic, homosexuality tended (and still tends) to face a greater stigma than virtually any other form of marginalization. Thus, one should not be too surprised at the reaction of many readers toward *AL*'s cover photo, and the fear and loathing it engendered.

Conclusions

Many, including Berninghausen, have argued that librarians must remain neutral on non-library issues and collect materials representing as many points of view as possible. Nowhere in any version of the Library Bill of Rights is there a statement to the effect that librarians must remain neutral. They, like everyone else, are largely products of the cultural ideologies and discourses in which they are immersed. As such, librarians are invested with their own ideological and cultural biases, and it is reasonable to assume that they will make judgments and decisions based on those biases. Neutrality is a form of fence-sitting, a form of silence. An attempt at complete neutrality constitutes, it seems to me, a complete surrender; a surrender to a Berninghausian orthodoxy that paradoxically detests the horrors perpetuated by humanity on itself and, at the same time, finds satisfaction in the maintenance of those horrors. Having a voice and using it to articulate deeply held convictions does not necessarily imply the silencing of other voices as Berninghausen would suggest. Socially responsible librarians do not reject the principles of intellectual freedom, they embrace those principles: "those who believe in the concept of social responsibility want to add the underground press to their collections, not toss out the traditional press" (Wedgeworth et al., 1973, p. 28). Indeed, many resources contain information outside the mainstream, but they are nowhere to be found in the standard reviewing and selection sources. Librarians must actively seek out alternative materials if they are to achieve anything that resembles a balanced collection.

Let us refer back again to the lesbian, gay, and bisexual population that was the catalyst for renewed debate. First, a small number of empirical studies have been completed to date that examine the information needs of homosexual populations. As Table 1 shows, the respondents of most of the studies considered libraries to be very important resources for information concerning homosexual orientation. By the same token, the respondents also found library service to be poor. Second, in their study of library selection, Sweetland and Christensen (1995) found that "regardless of comments and recommendations in reviews, ... [gay, lesbian, and bisexual] books are purchased by substantially fewer libraries that would be expected. This certainly suggests a possibility of ... bias on the part of librarians" (p. 39). Third, in their survey of 465 recent library school graduates, Carmichael and

Shontz (1996) found that "general issues of lesbigay status and questions about lesbigay materials in the library are by far the most volatile of issues" (p. 48). More importantly, he found that "whatever the claims of neutrality in professionalism, attitudes and perceptions are apparently affected by 'social orientation'. . . . along the liberal-conservative spectrum. . . . [M]uch as the respondents might seek an ideal neutrality, their professional attitudes are shaped by social forces" (p. 50). And what about the experiences of gay, lesbian, and bisexual librarians themselves? In 1970, Michael McConnell lost his job because he wished to marry his lover. ALA took up his cause, but

TABLE 1

Gay and Lesbian Perceptions of Resources and Services Provided by Libraries Concerning Homosexual Orientation

Year of Study	First Author	Number & Gender of Respondents	Importance of Library as Resource	Perception of Library Service
1990	Creelman	50 Females	Very Important	Poor
1993	Whitt	141 Females	Very Important	Poor
1997	Joyce	46 Males	Very Important	Poor
1999	Stenback	10 Females	Somewhat Important	Poor

after five years of virtual inaction, McConnell dropped the case in disgust (Carmichael, 1998; Gittings, 1990). For years, Jane Aldrich (1984), a school librarian, remained closeted, too fearful of losing her job to meet the needs of the gay student population. She felt most ashamed for not providing help to such students (p. 8). "Violet Clifford" [a pseudonym] (1997) describes the small British Columbia town where she works as a black hole: "My life as a librarian in this town has been marked by secrecy, subterfuge and vigilance" (p, 123). The point here is not to show that librarians of the far right dominate the profession, nor that all gay, lesbian, and bisexual librarians are forced into silence. The point is to show that the concept of neutrality is a myth. In a heterosexist and homophobic society, it is reasonable to expect that some librarians will also be heterosexist and homophobic. It is also reasonable to expect that some gay, lesbian, and bisexual librarians will remain closeted and withhold services from those in need. Neutrality does not exist in a vacuum; rather, it is immersed in a largely taken-for-granted and unquestioned status quo, and that status quo is certainly not neutral. If "neutral" librarians are also immersed in that status quo (or dominant ideology or hegemony or discursive formation or whichever phrasing you wish to employ), can they really be neutral?

It could be argued that the social responsibilities vs. neutrality debate is really nothing more than a red herring, and that all librarians, whatever their political persuasion, really want the same thing: equitable access to library materials for all. If this were really so, then why would a handful of progressive librarians be so intent on improving access to gay, lesbian, and bisexual people *at no one's expense*, and why would library services to such people be so poor in the first place?

In fact, user access constitutes a fundamental concern of socially responsible librarians. In a society that tends to stigmatize the margin, both publication of and access to alternative materials becomes and remains limited. "Neutral" librarians, by virtue of their silence, do little to promote effective access. Thus, "neutral" librarians help to perpetuate society's stigmatization of marginal populations. Thus, "neutral" librarians are not, in fact, neutral. Rather, they help to maintain an inequitable status quo created by and in the interests of the dominant forces within society; forces that must paradoxically define themselves by the Other while, at the same time, trying to destroy or subjugate or at least ignore that Other. Certainly one not need take a stand on every social issue, but those who sit on the fence ought to give some thought about who built that fence and why. By adopting a voice, librarians can then give voice to others who would not normally have one. The fence may never go away, but socially responsible librarians can help to construct a few gates.

APPENDIX I

COVER PHOTO
AMERICAN LIBRARIES
July/August 1992

APPENDIX II

LIBRARY BILL OF RIGHTS
Amended 1980

The American Library Association affirms that all libraries are forums for information and ideas, and that the following basic policies should guide their services.

1. Books and other library resources should be provided for the interest, information, and enlightenment of all people of the community the library serves. Materials should not be excluded because of the origin, background, or views of those contributing to their creation.

2. Libraries should provide materials and information presenting all points of view on current and historical issues. Materials should not be proscribed or removed because of partisan or doctrinal disapproval.

3. Libraries should challenge censorship in the fulfillment of their responsibility to provide information and enlightenment.

4. Libraries should cooperate with all persons and groups concerned with resisting abridgment of free expression and free access to ideas.

5. A person's right to use a library should not be denied or abridged because of origin, age, background, or views.

6. Libraries which make exhibit spaces and meeting rooms available to the public they serve should make such facilities available on an equitable basis, regardless of the beliefs or affiliations of individuals or groups requesting their use.

APPENDIX III

LIBRARY BILL OF RIGHTS
1939

Today indications in many parts of the world point to growing intolerance, suppression of free speech, and censorship affecting the rights of minorities and individuals. Mindful of this, the Council of the American Library Association publicly affirms its belief in the following basic policies which should govern the services of free public libraries.

1. Books and other reading matter selected for purchase from the public funds should be chosen because of value and interest to people of the community, and in no case should the selection be influenced by the race or nationality or the political or religious views of the writers.

2. As far as available material permits, all sides of questions on which differences of opinion exist should be represented fairly and adequately in the books and other reading matter purchased for public use.

3. The library as an institution to educate for democratic living should especially welcome the use of its meeting rooms for socially useful and cultural activities and the discussion of current public questions. Library meeting room should be available on equal terms to all groups in the community regardless of their beliefs or affiliations.

APPENDIX IV

LIBRARY BILL OF RIGHTS
Amended 1948

The Council of the American Library Association reaffirms its belief in the following basic policies which should govern the services of all libraries.

1. As a responsibility of library service, books and other reading matter selected should be chosen for values of interest, information and enlightenment of all the people of the community. In no case should any material be excluded because of race or nationality, or the political or religious views of the writer.

2. There should be the fullest practicable provision of material presenting all points of view concerning the problems and issues of our times, international, national, and local; and books or other reading matter of sound factual authority should not be proscribed or removed from library shelves because of partisan or doctrinal disapproval.

3. Censorship of books, urged or practiced by volunteer arbiters of morals or political opinion or by organizations that would establish a coercive concept of Americanism, must be challenged by libraries in maintenance of their responsibility to provide public information and enlightenment through the printed word.

4. Libraries should enlist the cooperation of allied groups in the fields of science, of education, and of book publishing in resisting all abridgment of the free access to ideas and full freedom of expression that are the tradition and heritage of Americans.

5. As an institution of education for democratic living, the library should welcome the use of its meeting rooms for socially useful and cultural activities and discussion of current public questions. Such meeting places should be available on equal

terms to all groups in the community regardless of the beliefs and affiliations of their members.

APPENDIX V

LIBRARY BILL OF RIGHTS
Amended 1967

The Council of the American Library Association reaffirms its belief in the following basic policies which should govern the services of all libraries.

1. As a responsibility of library service, books and other library materials selected should be chosen for values of interest, information and enlightenment of all people of the community. In no case should library materials be excluded because of the race or nationality or the social, political, or religious views of the authors.

2. Libraries should provide books and other materials presenting all points of view concerning the problems and issues of our times; no library materials should be proscribed or removed from libraries because of partisan or doctrinal disapproval.

3. Censorship should be challenged by libraries in the maintenance of their responsibility to provide public information and enlightenment.

4. Libraries should cooperate with all persons and groups concerned with resisting abridgment of free expression and free access to ideas.

5. The rights of an individual to use of a library should not be denied or abridged because of his [sic] age, race, religion, national origins or social or political views.

6. As an institution of education for democratic living, the library should welcome the use of its meeting rooms for socially

useful and cultural activities and discussion off current public questions. Such meeting places should be available on equal terms to all groups in the community regardless of the beliefs and affiliations of their members, provided that the meetings be open to the public.

Works Cited

ACONDA summary. (1970). *American Libraries, 1*, 685.

The ALAiad, or, a tale of two conferences. (1969). *Wilson Library Bulletin, 44*, 80-91.

Aldrich, J. (1984). Still here: An article about working in a public school library." *WLW Journal, 9*, 7-9.

Armitage, A. (1973). Social responsibility and the Library Bill of Rights: The Berninghausen debate [Response]. *Library Journal, 98*, 41.

Berman, S. (1981). The joy of cataloging: Essays, letters, reviews, and other explosions. Phoenix AZ: Oryx Press.

Berman, S., & Danky, J.P. (1984). Alternative library literature, 1982/1983: A biennial anthology. Phoenix, AZ: Oryx Press.

Berninghausen, D. K. (1953, June). The history of the ALA Intellectual Freedom Committee. *Wilson Library Bulletin, 27*, 813-7.

Berninghausen, D. K. (1972). Antithesis in librarianship: Social responsibility vs. the Library Bill of Rights. *Library Journal, 97*, 3675-81.

Berninghausen, D. K. (1970). The librarian's commitment to the Library Bill of Rights. *Library Trends, 19*, 19-38.

Berninghausen, D. K. (1975). The flight from reason: Essays on intellectual freedom in the academy, the press, and the library. Chicago: American Library Association.

Berry, J. (1969). The new constituency. *Library Journal, 94,* 2725-39.

Berry, J. (1970). ALA was the subject. *Library Journal, 95,* 2613-22.

Berry, J., Fialkoff, F., St. Lifer, E., & Rogers, M. 1993. Under protest: ALA Midwinter Meeting in Denver. *Library Journal, 118*(4), 35-6.

Brace, W. (1992). Reader forum [Letter]. *American Libraries, 23,* 738.

Buschman, J., Rosenzweig, M., & Harger, E. (1994). The clear imperative for involvement: Librarians must address social issues. *American Libraries, 25,* 575-6.

Business – not quite as usual: ALA Conference, Kansas City, June 23-29 – A report on the council and membership meetings and the president's inaugural speech. (1968). *Library Journal, 93,* 2797-2809.

Carmichael, J.V. (1997). A gauntlet for all reasons. In N. G. Kester [Ed.], *Liberating minds: The stories and professional lives of gay, lesbian, and bisexual librarians and their advocates,* (pp. 9-22). Jefferson, NC: McFarland & Company.

Carmichael, J.V. (1998, August). *Homosexuality and United States libraries: Land of the free, but not home to the gay.* Paper presented at 64th IFLA General Conference. Retrieved August 25, 2007 from http://www.ifla.org/IV/ifla64/002-138e.

Carmichael, J.V. & Shontz, M.L. (1996). The last socially acceptable prejudice: Gay and lesbian issues, social responsibilities, and coverage of these topics in M.L.I.S./M.L.S. programs. *Library Quarterly, 66,* 21-58

Chatman, E. A. (1985a). Information, mass media use and the working poor. *Library and Information Science Research, 7,* 97-113.

Chatman, E. A. (1985b). Low income and leisure: Implications for public library use. *Public Libraries, 24,* 34-6.

Chatman, E. A. (1987a). Opinion leadership, poverty, and information sharing. *RQ, 26,* 341-53.

Chatman, E. A. (1987b). The information world of low-skilled workers. *Library and Information Science Research, 9,* 265-83.

Clearances [Editorial]. (1993, February 15). *New Yorker,* p. 4, 6.

Clifford, V. (1997). A lesbian librarian in the hinterland. In Norman G. Kester (Ed.),
Liberating minds: The stories and professional lives of gay, lesbian, and bisexual librarians and their advocates (pp. 123-125). Jefferson, NC: McFarland & Company.

Creelman, J. A. E. & Harris, R. (1990). Coming out: The information needs of lesbians.
Collection Building, 10, 37-41.

Gaughan, T. (1992). The last socially acceptable prejudice [Editorial]. *American Libraries,* 23, 612.

Geller, E. (1969). Crisis in red and black. *Library Journal, 94,* 3134-3138.

Gittings, B. (1990). Gays in library land: The Gay and Lesbian Task Force of the American Library Association: The first sixteen years. Philadelphia: Barbara Gittings.

Gough, C. & Greenblatt, E. [Eds.] (1990). *Gay and lesbian library service.* Jefferson, NC: McFarland & Company.

Greenblatt, E. (1990). Homosexuality: The evolution of a concept in the Library of Congress Subject Headings. In C. Gough & E. Greenblatt [Eds.], *Gay and lesbian library service* (pp. 75-101). Jefferson, NC: McFarland & Company.

Guidelines for librarians interacting with South Africa. (1989, September). *SRRT Newsletter, 93,* 7-9.

Harris, R. M. (1988). The information needs of battered women. *RQ, 28,* 62-70.

Hartwell, R. (1992). Reader forum [Letter]. *American Libraries, 23,* 843.

Jordan, P. (1975, April). Librarians and social commitment. *Assistant Librarian, 68,* 62-66.

Josey, E.J. (1973). Social responsibility and the Library Bill of Rights: The Berninghausen debate [Response]." *Library Journal, 98,* 32-3.

Joyce, S. & Schrader, A M. (1997). Hidden perceptions: Edmonton gay males and the
Edmonton Public Library. Canadian Journal of Information and Library Science, 22(April), 19-37.

Kopkind, A. (1993). The gay moment. *The Nation, 256*(17), 577-86.

Leita, C. (1983). Booked for civil disobedience: A librarian's story. *WLW Journal, 8,* 47-51.

MacCann, D. (1989). Introduction. In D. MacCann (Ed.), *Social responsibility in librarianship: Essays on equality.* Jefferson, NC: McFarland.

Malice toward some [Editorial]. (1993, October 26). *New Yorker,* p. 4, 6.

Martin, B. (1980). Social intervention by libraries. *Library Association Record, 82,* 417.

Michell, W.W. (1992). Reader forum [Letter]. *American Libraries, 23,* 843.

Nelson, J. A. (1987). The Congress for Change. In M. L. Bundy & F.J. Stielow [Eds.], *Activism in American librarianship, 1962-1973* (pp. 123-133). New York: Greenwood Press.

New directions. (1970). *American Libraries, 1*, 938-40.

Office for Intellectual Freedom , [Comp.]. (1992). *Intellectual freedom manual*. Chicago: American Library Association.

On the move in San Francisco: Annual conference wrap-up [Cover page]. (1992). *American Libraries, 23*(July/August).

Raymond, B. (1979). ACONDA and ANACONDA revisited: A retrospective glance at the sounds of fury of the sixties. *Journal of Library History, 14*(Summer), 349-62.

Rasimus, E.J. (1992). Reader forum [Letter]. *American Libraries, 23*, 625.

Recommendations from ACONDA: A report by the ALA Ad Hoc Council Committee on ACONDA for consideration of Council, Midwinter Meeting, January 1971. (1971). *American Libraries, 2*, 93-6.

Robbins, L. S. (1994). The Library of Congress and the Federal Loyalty Programs, 1947-1956: No "Communists or cocksuckers." *Library Quarterly, 64*(4), 365-85.

Robbins, L. S. (1996). Champions of a cause: American librarians and the Library Bill of Rights in the 1950s. *Library Trends, 45*(1), 28-49.

Samek, T. (1996). The Library Bill of Rights in the 1960s: One profession, one ethic. *Library Trends, 45*(1), 50-60.

Schrader, A. M. (1997). Community pressures to censor gay and lesbian materials in the public libraries of Canada. In N. G. Kester (Ed.), *Liberating minds: The stories of gay, lesbian, and bisexual librarians and their advocates* (pp. 149-160). Jefferson, NC: McFarland.

Schuman, P. G. (1976). *Social responsibilities and libraries: A Library Journal/School Library Journal selection*. New York: R. R. Bowker.

Stenback, T. & Schrader, A. M. (1999). Venturing from the closet: A qualitative study of the information needs of lesbians. *Public Library Quarterly*, 17, 37-50.

Stevens, D. (1989). Social responsibility and librarianship: A dilemma of professionalism. *Canadian Library Journal*, 46, 17-22.

Sweetland, J. H. & Christensen, P. G. (1995). Gay, lesbian and bisexual titles: Their treatment in the review media and their selection by libraries. *Collection Building*, 14, 32-41.

Taylor, H. (1968). Society and revolution: An educator examines the relevance of education to the realities of a radically changing society. *Library Journal*, 93, 509-12.

Uricchio, W. (1994). Telescopic philanthropy: How much social responsibility is too much? *American Libraries*, 25, 574, 576.

Velleman, R. A. (1979). Serving physically disabled people: An information handbook for all libraries. New York: R. R. Bowker.

Wedgeworth, R., et al. (1973). Social responsibility and the Library Bill of Rights: The Berninghausen debate. *Library Journal*, 98, 25-41.

Winter, M. L. (1983). Taming the technological beast: The debate on nuclear education. *School Library Journal*, 30, 36-40.

Whitt, A. J. (1993). The information needs of lesbians. *Library and Information Science Research*, 15, 275-89.

Witt, J.M. (1992). Reader forum [Letter]. *American Libraries*, 23, 625.

[This is an updated and expanded version of the article "A Few Gates: An Examination of the Social Responsibilities Debate in the Early 1970s and 1990s" which appeared in *Progressive Librarian*, No. 15, Winter 1998/1999.]

(Illustration reproduced with the kind permission of *American Libraries*.)

Activist Librarianship: Heritage or Heresy?

By Ann Sparanese

Thank you for inviting me to speak here today. I am extremely honored to be here at your school. When your colleague Bill Kenz first emailed me last fall about doing a talk for your lecture series here, I was extremely surprised. I told him, "I'm really not on the speakers' circuit." He said that was okay. Since I am *not* on the speaker's circuit and know that I am a poor substitute for someone like Michael Moore, I naturally have been mulling over this talk for a good long while, trying to figure out what it is that you would want to hear from me and what it is that I might have to say to you—many of you are my librarian colleagues and some of you are students and professors. It's been over a year since I wrote that little email to fellow and sister librarians that is credited with "saving" Michael Moore's book, *Stupid White Men and Other Sorry Excuses for the State of the Nation*.

But the story of the "lone" librarian has continued to be of interest out there; last week I even got a call from a BBC reporter who wanted to do an interview because the book has won some kind of award in England. The success of Moore's new documentary film, *Bowling for Columbine*, seems to generate even more traction for this human interest item. My absolute favorite headline of all the news and feature pieces that have been written comes from the paper *In These Times*. Their short piece was titled "Librarian Saves Stupid White Men." I suppose the story resonates with people because it seems that librarians do not have the reputation of being fighters, troublemakers, or activists. Maybe folks just never expected a librarian to be involved with a book as iconoclastic as *Stupid White Men*. I think the public might still think of librarians as passive keepers of the books. But in the library circles I travel in, that image could not be further from the truth.

We all know why you have invited me here today. "It's all got to do with that book! That book and nothing else!" For a year and a half, I kid you not, I have sincerely tried hard, without success, to play down the role that little email of mine played in the story of that book! But that story has fascinated reporters and, to a lesser degree, librarians everywhere, who have now been catapulted into the spotlight as heroes and, as Michael Moore now is fond of saying, "revolutionaries"! I must say, that crack by Moore—which he likes to repeat in all his interviews—that when we are all sitting behind desks shushing people it's really because we are plotting the revolution—tickles the heck out of me. I personally *do* think that librarians have been, and continue to be, heroes and revolutionaries and "small d" democrats in the fullest sense of the word. But I don't think my little email is the best example of that. And I must state, here and now, that my involvement with Michael Moore's book is the first and last time I ever intend to save *any* stupid white men!

I was mulling over some of this stuff in bed a week ago with one of my four, relatively pacifist cats sitting near my head as I was just waking up. I was pondering the "how to start," "can I be funny" questions when an ear-piercing yowl went up, my most timid cat raced across the bed, and in her path was my *face*. My first thoughts were, as the blood ran down my cheek, that now I not only have to be funny, but I will have to do it with a cat scratches across my face—giving a whole new meaning to one way I like to think of myself: the "scrappy" librarian. I assure you that my encounters as an activist librarian have been non-physical, mostly oral or written in nature! I did once have a long knock down, drag out union battle against a library director, because I am a union shop steward in our library. At that time I was known to have said that when it was over only *one* of us would still be standing. But that was merely figurative. At no time did a cat fight ensue (although a court fight did). And P.S., it was *me* left standing!

This is all to say that I have been an activist all my life, wherever I happened to find myself. I define activist to mean a person who believes in engaging in the struggle for progressive social change, for the expansion of democracy, peace, and justice. The true irony for me in all this business surrounding the release of Michael Moore's book is that, although I have been an activist woman for most of my adult life and an activist librarian for more fifteen years, the stuff I have worked on, and consider to be important, worthwhile, and genuine contributions have garnered very little recognition. Or even negative recognition. This is very normal. Considering that I am the adversarial union shop steward at the Englewood Public Library, you can imagine that as far as my library's board is concerned—with a couple of exceptions—they are not anxious to sing my praises. That might be a bad precedent come contract time! What happened with the Michael Moore book was a fluke—one of those little seeds that a person plants at the right moment which actually bears abundant fruit of an exotic kind! Any gardener knows what I mean. Sometimes it comes from those little seeds you disregarded as soon as you threw them into the ground. You are surprised and delighted when they produce something fantastic—while the stuff you sweated over only get the ordinary results or no results at all.

I've printed up copies of my original email about the book. I'm surprised I even saved it, although I do have a habit of being a bit of a perfectionist when casting my opinions out into cyberspace. When I sent this email message to two library listserves, I had no idea that it would have any effect at all. In fact, it is a testimony to how little interest I thought other librarians would have in this that I did not even send this email to the listserves read daily by American Librarian Association (ALA) Council members or to Member-Forum (another ALA listserve) or even to PUBLIB, a list read by a vast number of public librarians. I sent it to two lists populated by librarians and library workers "left of center," those considered "activist librarians." And maybe even querulous, trouble-making librarians. Those would be the listserve of the ALA's Social Responsibilities Round Table Action Council, and the Progressive Librarians Guild, an independent group of which I am a dues-paying member. Now *here* would be some folks who are interested in this, I thought, and they might even know who Michael Moore is! And anyway, I felt that I was just doing my duty to report what Michael Moore had stated a day or two earlier at a meeting of the New Jersey Citizen Action organization, where he was the keynote speaker. To my knowledge no other librarian had been there to hear what was going to happen to Michael Moore's book.

I didn't actually know that Michael Moore was scheduled to speak there. I vaguely knew that he had a new book coming out, because I remembered placing it on pre-publication order at our library. I was at the meeting of the New Jersey Citizen Action group in the first place because of another aspect of my life in which I consider myself to be an activist, as I have already mentioned—that of the trade union movement. I am the trustee of the New Jersey Citizen Action, appointed to that position by the Bergen County Central Trades and Labor Council. Central labor councils, in case folk do not know, are local groups which bring together all the unions affiliated with the AFL-CIO in a given geographical area. So that is why I was there and why I heard Michael Moore despondently tell the group of about 100 assembled that his new book, *Stupid White Men,* was definitely getting axed by his publisher, HarperCollins. He said that it would never be published and that we at that gathering would probably be the only people to see or hear any parts of this book. And so he read us some of the juicier parts, including his open letter to the President. I think of myself as a person who "questions authority," but Michael Moore takes questioning authority to a whole other level! He also told the audience that he didn't want them to "do" anything about this situation, that there were more pressing problems to attend to. But the trouble was, I am a librarian and this didn't sound like such good advice to me. Furthermore, this was a large public gathering and no one was sworn to secrecy, least of all me. I was constitutionally unable to follow his leadership on this. I knew what *I* had to do, small and fruitless as it seemed at the time. I had to tell my colleagues what was "up" with HarperCollins.

That was Saturday, December 1, 2001. On Monday I sent the email. As you can see yourselves, it was a pretty much verbatim report of what went on at the meeting. I wrote, proofed, and pressed "send." And then, quite honestly I must tell you, I *forgot* about it! I did not "orchestrate" or "organize" a darn thing beyond notifying my erstwhile colleagues about the situation. Although I only heard from a few people about it, it must have gotten picked up by others who sent it around, and it definitely was picked up and reprinted by a wonderful little 'zine on the web called "Library Juice," edited by a young librarian named Rory Litwin. Lots of folks read Library Juice and some of them are bigger troublemakers than me, because a few days later, according to Michael Moore, HarperCollins was calling him complaining about receiving "hate mail" from librarians. I'm positive that was an exaggeration, though I don't know if it was by Moore or by HarperCollins.

I know your publicity says that I organized a "letter-writing" campaign. It really didn't happen that way—and I've corrected Michael Moore when he says I went into librarian "chatrooms" as well. (*What* librarian chat rooms?) I wasn't even thinking of organizing an email campaign to HarperCollins—although looking back on it now, someone should have done that!! If I was formulating any kind of action at all, I was focused on the fact that in a month the American Library Association would be having its midwinter conference in New Orleans and HarperCollins would undoubtedly have a large presence there in the exhibits area. If I was thinking of anything, it was that we would get a group together and go to visit HarperCollins and say, "What gives? Why did you censor Michael Moore's new book?" But we never got to do that, because in January, before the conference, I got a call from a reporter from Salon.com asking me if I was happy about the news about Michael Moore's book. I said I didn't know what the news was and she told me that the book was being released and it was because of librarians and my email to them. I was more than shocked. But, sure, I was pleased! And there (or maybe it was on Holt Uncensored) began the urban legend of the "lone librarian" who saved Michael Moore's book from the recycle machine.

But of course it was nothing of the kind. Rather it was a rare, lovely, delicious, and relatively easy victory gained through the collective action of librarians in defense of one of our core values, opposition to censorship in all its forms. Librarians, as an integral part of our professional commitment, take censorship seriously and generally fight it where we find it. In this case, it was directly at the publisher's door. As you probably know by now, HarperCollins wanted Moore to rewrite objectionable parts of the book and pay for the reprinting. They thought the book inappropriately criticized the President in the months following a terrorist attack and wanted that criticism and its tone to be drastically altered.

Think about it—what would make a publisher, a corporation, take big money already invested in printing and sales (through prepublication orders) and toss it into a paper shredder? A government order? But HarperCollins never claimed there was any such order. This form of censorship that went *against* the company's bottom line of profit (the reason the company exists, after all) could only be motivated by the fear of seeming unpatriotic. To me this was a stunning admission and extremely worrisome. I suppose the publisher honestly believed that public opinion would not only guarantee failure of this book, but that they were haunted by the specter of public disapproval tainting future releases of other books on their list. I think it must have been "fear," pure and simple, and wanting desperately to remain in the mainstream of what HarperCollins calculated to be overwhelmingly pro-government public opinion after the events of September 11.

Why was the attempted self-censorship by HarperCollins so significant, as I saw it that morning in New Brunswick? To tell you the truth, I was quite affected by what Michael Moore was telling us. Being from the New York City area, I knew the effects of September 11 on the psyche of the city and the country. A pall had hung over our area of the country for, I would say, two months before people were truly smiling again. The country was at war in Afghanistan by December, and the USA PATRIOT Act had been passed with virtually no discussion in Congress. But that was government stuff. The government always attempts to censor and repress in time of war. But the government had apparently not taken any particular interest in *Stupid White Men*. This was the publishing house itself who decided to "pulp" the book and all its investments in it! This was an action—as Michael Moore himself pointed out—against the publisher's own bottom line: profit. Profit, not patriotism, is supposed to be the bottom line of the new global economy. So this was truly chilling. Of course they proposed recouping some of those losses by asking Moore to rewrite the offensive passages (had to be most of the book—this is really offensive political criticism) and then pay for it, but by December they must have figured out that that was not going to happen. So—they were willing to just eat it and that would be that.

I do remember thinking—hey, this is Michael Moore, not some unknown first time-author! There are books that *never* will see the light of day by new, less powerful, less revenue-generating authors. This was serious business, which is why when Moore advised the audience to "do nothing" about the situation, I couldn't pay him any mind at all. This was bigger than Michael Moore and more important than just his book. This is why I wrote the email.

The rest is a history you all know. When HarperCollins finally released the book in February, they grossly miscalculated what the public response would be. They told Moore the book would die an ignominious death and that they would organize no book tours for him. A couple of weeks after it was released, it hit the *New York Times* Best Sellers list. And it's still there today. Even with everything that has happened and is happening in our nation, the book struck a deep reservoir of mistrust and truth-seeking on the part of the American people. Not to mention that they like to laugh and this is a funny, funny book about the most serious of problems. While not the best book written on contemporary politics and, some have said, full of hyperbole and maybe even some bad stats, the book has tapped into the desires of the people to hear it told another way than it is the daily press. I think they like the class (as in working class) approach. Despite everything, people of the United States still do connect to politics and treasure dissent even in the most difficult times. This is what the commercial success of *Stupid White Men* means to me.

In the course of last year, some colleagues started suggesting nominating me for intellectual freedom awards. This was something I absolutely had to nip in the bud, because activism in defense of intellectual freedom can be serious business indeed and usually has unpleasant repercussions—not happy-face stories in the newspapers. In librarianship, unbeknownst to the public and almost equally unknown to most librarians, there is a long and hallowed history of activism both in the interest of intellectual freedom and in the service of social responsibilities in libraries. Librarians have lost the jobs they loved, their reputations have been besmirched, and their incomes have been sacrificed in defense of the principles embodied in the right to read, and in the Library Bill of Rights. I was not one of these, and take no credit as a champion of intellectual freedom, at least not in this case. I wrote an email that helped provide us with one small, sweet victory and brought attention to the sometimes powerful role of librarians in our society.

What these events really speak to is the power of collective action by librarians in anything they might set their minds to. It testifies to the fact that librarians are important to publishers and that we can help them to do the right thing. By doing so we enrich our society, live our professional values, and help our nation to live up to its true values.

Your generous invitation to speak to you today gave me a reason to think more deeply about librarianship, about how there is a strand of its history that is activist involvement with important issues of the day, censorship being only one among them. It has made me interested in studying the history and policies of the American Library Association and the history of my colleagues in the defense of many democratic values, including civil liberties and diversity. Over time librarians have been willing to engage in activism surrounding our values, not merely to propagate a neutral stand in the face of threats to democracy. This has been a dynamic in our profession. I learned far more than I am able to share in this talk today.

I didn't become a librarian to do activist stuff. I didn't become a librarian in order to find a venue for my commitment to social change, although as a citizen, I had been active in movements for social change. I became a librarian because I though it was a salutary profession, good for our society in some vague and general way, but mostly because I was tired of waiting tables with a college degree and it was definitely time to get off the Mommy track. I had no grand notions of doing much more than serving my own diverse community in some undefined but positive way. I didn't even take a course on intellectual freedom class in library school—it wasn't required. I had no idea that my previous life of activism and engagement (being a child of the 1960s, the anti-war movement, a Cuba enthusiast, etc.) could somehow ever spill over into my life as a librarian, and to tell you the truth, it didn't for a number of years.

I think I started to make the connection when I realized that my library—in which I was simply a rank-and-file librarian (which I still am today though I manage a six-person reference staff)—was not really serving the whole of our community. Despite the fact that the official census in 1990 reported that our town was almost 40% African American, our library's collection of materials about contemporary Black life, Black writers, and Black history and contemporary issues was severely lacking. It didn't take me too long to figure out that this needed to change. I didn't see anyone else around who saw the need to change it, though we were a building full of good, solid librarians and nice people and lots of books. I realized that I could write a grant for enough money to change the situation. This was in the days when the New Jersey State Library had grant money to give away—not like today when state libraries and state budgets are under siege. This obviously was *not* in my job description. I won the grant and bought lots of books, even the most controversial ones. I convened, through advertisements and news stories, a Community Advisory Committee to help build the collection by soliciting what community members wanted for the collection. This was so successful that I repeated the process with Hispanic collections and outreach services, and with a collection and outreach campaign built around labor studies—an esoteric subject even in the union-dense state I live in. With each new project, the idea of library activism—in this case, the idea of community outreach and service—informed my work. Although it seems so obvious to me and maybe it does to you too, you would be amazed at how it often just is not done.

I think this is sometimes because the concept of activism or advocacy is seen as contrary to the idea of neutralism or neutrality in libraries. That is, that it is not the role of libraries or librarians to promote or advocate, but rather to sit back and in a professional manner provide neutral, unbiased access to information. But I would argue that few activities in this human existence of ours are unbiased and neutral. Although my involvement with Michael Moore's book is viewed mainly as a victory for intellectual freedom, I would not define my brand of activism as having solely to do with this one ethic of libraries in a democratic society. Library activism for me has had to do with the social responsibilities of libraries, not a purist version of intellectual freedom. The role of libraries, in my opinion, is the active promotion of democratic and pluralist ideas. Our absolute obligation is to seek out and acquire materials, as the Library Bill of Rights says, of all points of view on current and historical issues. And as the ALA policy manual says very clearly, "to become involved in the issues of the day which impact upon libraries and library services." Now, I ask you, in an information society are there very many issues that will *not* impact upon libraries?

Not all librarians agree with this concept although it is actually enshrined, to some degree, in the mission and policy statements of the American Library Association, primarily because of the struggles about it that took place during the 1960s and 1970s. Should librarianship become involved in the great issues of the day, or remain a profession aloof in the abstract world that thinks of intellectual freedom in the most idealized, purist fashion? Libraries, by all means, were not the only institutions where this issue was raised and debated. The role of the Supreme Court, for instance, also continues to have this contradiction—should it be an activist court or simply a court of the interpretation of the words of the founders? Is advocacy in journalism a betrayal of the profession or its actual purpose, if one admits to the fact that completely unbiased journalism could only be practiced by robots? Almost every journalist advocates something, even if it is simple acceptance of the words of the government. Support of the status quo is not neutrality.

I called this talk today "Activist Librarianship: Heritage or Heresy" because of the history of this question in librarianship. It would take a much longer paper for a much more involved presentation to really plumb the depths of this debate over the years. I believe that the librarian's devotion to democracy and democratic values often requires an activism that goes beyond lip service to abstract principles and involves the nitty gritty of how such principles play out in the society. This dialectic has encompassed many years and many individuals' battles; perhaps the greatest of these occurred during the 1960s and 1970s when, like in every other arena in U.S. society, values were being questioned, and the great battles around civil rights and the Vietnam War were being fought. Activist librarians were in there from the git-go. It wasn't until I began to do the research for this talk that I realized the really deep roots that activist librarianship has, and that it parallels activism in American life in general.

For the librarians in this audience especially, I have prepared a bibliography of the books I have found that document this history. I really do believe that, as historian Howard Zinn, author of *A People's History of the United States*, says "If you don't know history, it's like you were born yesterday."

Many of these books are biographies of activist librarians. They often found themselves embroiled in struggles around intellectual freedom, but not only intellectual freedom. There was Miss Ruth Brown, the 30-year director of Bartlesville Public Library in Oklahoma, who found herself forced to resign in 1951, ostensibly because she refused to remove *The Nation* and books about the Soviet Union from her library shelves. But the reality is that Miss Ruth Brown was involved in something far more subversive: in her life as a citizen she was a member of the Oklahoma branch of the Congress of Racial Equality (CORE) and practiced racial equality in her personal and professional life. This was the real reason why Miss Brown lost her job. She was not neutral on the question of racial equality.

There was E.J. Josey, the great African-American librarian from Georgia who, because of his race, was denied membership in his state librarian association. Despite the facts that segregation existed in southern libraries, Black librarians were denied membership in the state library associations of four southern states, and substandard service for Blacks existed in most of the libraries of the north, not one word was written about these issues in the library press between 1936 and 1959, until the iconoclastic and activist editor of *Library Journal*, Eric Moon, took up the fight. E.J. Josey and others like him believed that without respect for basic human rights, free and equal access to information and culture cannot be achieved. Therefore the role of the librarian, as the role of the citizen, was to concern him or herself as a professional, with human rights as well as abstract principles such as intellectual freedom. The kind of changes that E.J. Josey brought about for libraries and librarianship is a testament to the doggedness of his devotion to the social responsibilities of libraries. Josey is still living, and despite the fact that his struggle within the American Library Association has been a long and bitter one, he did become its president, and has been honored with a lifetime membership. He is truly a leader of the civil and human rights movement in this country. I mentioned Eric Moon, who was editor of *Library Journal* for nine years. Moon said, "I believe that libraries are involved in society per se, and that actions such as Vietnam involve libraries. I believe that war affects libraries. I believe that racism affects libraries." He helped carry out these struggles on the pages of the *Journal*, which in turn encouraged the activist forces within the American Library Association. Beginning with a stand against racial segregation, the organization representing American libraries would eventually take "the unprecedented action of denouncing a war." The legacy of that period is still seen in the policy manual of the American Library Association, and in the resolutions that come forth at every session of its governing body. The struggle between concern for strictly "traditional" library issues and a broad view of the role of the library and librarians in society seems to be played out continuously—at least as long as I have been in the profession and long before. For me, the activist, social responsibility argument has great potency, because slavishness to neutrality can often simply be a mask to support the status quo. But the status quo has, can, and does deprive millions of Americans of the kind of rights that are required for full intellectual freedom. This was Josey's message. So librarians have to be involved in the process to make those rights realities.

But not everyone believes that. Those that say that librarians, as librarians, should only be involved in the narrowest of library-related issues still mostly get their way in the American Library Association. I consider myself in the Moon school of library activism. He said, "Libraries had a simple choice: to be a significant thread in the social fabric, an active participant in social change or to face an inevitable passage toward irrelevance, possible extinction or a existence as some kind of grey historical relic." Socially responsible librarianship is librarianship that is part of—not dissociated from—society and its needs, problems, and concerns. Intellectual freedom is not the only ethic of the profession of librarianship and it is not a purist value, separated from other democratic principles and human rights.

There was also Zoia Horn, a reference librarian at Bucknell University who was jailed for her principled refusal to testify at the conspiracy trial of the Harrisburg Seven in 1972. There was an informer who worked in Zoia's library at Bucknell, an ex-convict sent there by the FBI. This informer implicated other library personnel in a fabricated "conspiracy" and later, though given immunity from self-incrimination, Zoia refused to testify because she objected to the idea that libraries could become places of infiltration, spying, and aggressive government action against the peace movement. She went to jail for 20 days for contempt of court, although it could have been three months if the trial had not been cut short. The American Library Association did not come to her support, because there was conflict there about whether she was doing these things "as a librarian" and whether she was correct in doing so.

My talk here today is not just about history and definitely not just about a single email, as powerful as that might have been. Zoia's run-in with a planted spy has a particular resonance today for the situations that librarians are finding themselves placed in with the passage of the USA PATRIOT Act. As most of you probably know, this huge piece of legislation passed both houses of Congress with almost no discussion in October 2001. Some of the elements of this law include the cancellation of habeus corpus for non-citizens; expanded government wiretap ability; the authorization of secret searches; new rules for seizure of library and bookstore records; the monitoring of conversation between lawyers and clients; CIA spying on American citizens; the possible designation of domestic groups as terrorists; lowering the threshold for obtaining a search warrant from probable cause to "ongoing criminal investigation;" and the institution of military tribunals for anyone called a "suspected terrorist" by the President. The American Civil Liberties Union (ACLU) maintains that sections of this law are blatantly unconstitutional. Despite this, only one senator (Feingold) voted against this bill and in the House of Representatives, only 66 members voted against it.

Section 215 of this law specifically grants the government the right to obtain library and bookstore records in secret without proving that a crime has been committed. Librarians presented with such a warrant under the USA PATRIOT Act are forbidden to discuss it anyone except a lawyer. They are forbidden to discuss it with the patron whose records may be sought, despite the fact that the patron may have committed no crime, or a crime may not even have been committed. I suspect that most library users have no idea that their records—for instance, of internet use or books checked out—may be obtained in such a manner and with such utter secrecy. After much debate, the American Library Association passed a resolution opposing this law at its meeting in January 2003, followed by several state library associations. It does not call for the repeal or elimination of unconstitutional sections, but rather their amendment or change. It is not the strongest resolution and was not hastily adopted. But it was activist librarians who demanded discussion, who led the way in this work of crafting a resolution that would pass the governing body—librarians who feel compelled to defend the Bill of Rights and to advocate against the passage of legislations that erodes our basic freedoms and due process rights.

There is new law that is coming down the pike, nicknamed PATRIOT II. The details of this legislation were leaked out. The article that broke the story says that the administration is holding back proposing it until Congress is in a vulnerable state of fear—for instance if and when we are in a war against Iraq—and the risk of terrorist reprisals is high. It's called the Domestic Security Enhancement Act of 2003 (DSEA), and grants the Attorney General almost unbridled powers in a wide arena of law enforcement. It authorizes secret arrests. It allows local and state police to spy on citizens. It even puts citizenship itself in jeopardy—and I am not talking about the citizenship of the naturalized, I'm talking about the citizenship of the native-born American. Section 501 of DSEA would allow the federal government to strip the citizenship of an American citizen if the person provided "material support" to a group that the United States has designated as a terrorist organization. I don't know if this particular legislation mentions libraries in the specific way that the USA PATRIOT Act did. But I would hope—and I'll be in there fighting for—our professional association to take as strong a stand as it possibly can against it. Libraries are a cornerstone of democracy, but without all of the other cornerstones, guarantees, rights, and liberties that make up a democracy, how powerful a force can libraries or information ever be?

Sooner or later, I suspect there will be a librarian who will refuse to provide information or who will reveal the requests of the FBI to the press. Hopefully, the ALA will come to her or his defense. But it is clear that the activist librarians will be right there, I can assure you.

Many of the rights and liberties we Americans have taken for granted with regard to information seeking are threatened in the new political climate. The impending war against Iraq threatens libraries—everybody with any common sense can see that when money is spent for bombs and war, it cannot be used for institutions such as libraries. All our social programs will suffer. People of the United States will continue to go without adequate medical insurance. Just the other day, Florida Governor Jeb Bush, in justifying his gutting of the Florida State Library, said that money cannot be found for everything, war takes money away from other priorities. Although war is not good for libraries, librarians at the ALA refused to take a stand to urge the President to continue with the inspection process rather than seeking unilateral war. I put forth this resolution at ALA Council and I regret the outcome, because I don't see how the democracy that librarians believe in cannot be compromised by the events that accompany a war. Not that I think the only reason this war should be opposed by librarians as librarians is simply because of budget considerations. It is because this war, and the political climate that has given rise to an Administration that is promulgating the idea of preemptive, unending war, is a threat to our democracy. The Bill of Rights is being shredded and so is Article I, Sect ion 8 of the Constitution which says that only Congress may declare war.

There was a compelling essay in the October, 2002 issue of *Library Journal* entitled "Can Libraries Save Democracy?" by a Texas librarian named Michael Baldwin. He argues that in order to be institutions of democracy, libraries must promote democracy and an informed citizenry as its main, most important mission. And I would hope that the public would value this inherent purpose and demand it of their public libraries—not just their providing folks with the latest novels.

Baldwin says in his think piece: "If informed citizenship had been the primary goal of libraries over the past 50 years, America might be a much different country. People would be better informed about political issues. Grass-roots activism would be an integral social activity. The right to vote would be understood as an almost sacred privilege exercised by an informed citizenry. Politicians would work for the public good because citizens would not tolerate undue political influence by special interests." He ends with this idea: "The American public library is the most important invention of our democratic society after the Constitution itself. Libraries can provide the social leverage to return America to a democratic destiny. We will be condemned by history and by ourselves if we allow democracy to perish."

When I heard Michael Moore say his book was going to be scrapped, I didn't have all this stuff on my mind, at least not consciously. But when you asked me to come and talk about it today, I realize that this was the reason all along for that little email. Thank you for letting me share my ideas with you today.

["Activist Libriaanship: Heritage or Heresy" was originally presented as part of the second annual Livingston Lord Library Lecture Series at Minnesota State University, Moorhead, on March 10, 2003. A slightly different version of the speech appeared in *Progressive Librarian*, No. 22, Summer 2003.]

Activist Librarianship: Heritage or Heresy? One Librarian's Two-Part List of Relevant and Thoughtful Reading for the Engaged Librarian and the Involved Citizen

Compiled by Ann Sparanese
Especially for the Librarians among Us:
Librarians and Social Responsibilities

> Neutral institutions perpetrate such social ills as racism and sexism. They don't go around advocating that blacks and women be denied equal rights and libraries don't brag that their collections contain nothing but the story of John Q. Wasp...but burying one's prejudices in a bureaucracy does not qualify one as neutral. Mary McKenney, 1971.

> The broad social responsibilities of the American Library Association are defined in terms of the contributions that librarianship can make in ameliorating or solving the critical problems of society; support for efforts to help inform and educate the people of the United States on these problems and to encourage them to examine the many views on the facts regarding each problem; and the willingness of ALA to take a position on current critical issues with the relationship to libraries and library service set forth in the position statement. ALA Handbook of Organization, 2002-2003

Abdullahi, I. (1992). *E.J. Josey: An activist librarian.* Metuchen, NJ: Scarecrow Press. E.J. Josey believed in the connection between libraries and human rights. This series of essays by librarians who were influenced by him reveals the vast contributions that he made to librarianship.

Bundy, M. L. & and Stielow, F. J. (1987). *Activism in American librarianship, 1962-1973.* New York, Greenwood Press. A collection of articles by librarians, who, with the exception of one, were all deeply involved in the movements of the "sixties."

Everything You Always Wanted to Know about Sandy Berman But Were Afraid to Ask. (1995). Jefferson, NC: McFarland. Minnesota's own pioneer in cataloging for the people is celebrated with a series of essays.

Horn, Z. (1995). *Zoia! Memoirs of Zoia Horn, battler for freedom.* Jefferson, NC: Mc Farland & Co. Perhaps Zoia is best known for going to jail for her refusal to testify in the Harrisburg Seven conspiracy case in 1972. But her experiences as chair of ALA's Intellectual Freedom Committee in 1976-1977 also make illuminating historical reading.

Josey, E.J. (Ed.). (1970). *The black librarian in America.* Metuchen, NJ: Scarecrow. The thoughts, experiences and perspectives of African Americans in librarianship are brought together here by one of their exemplary practicioners.

Kister, K. F. (2002). *Eric Moon: The life and library times.* Jefferson, NC: Mcfarland. Moon was ALA president in 1976-77, but what led to that was Moon's struggle inside the ALA for social responsibility. This biography conveys the spirit of the times, the tumult inside the association over such touchstone American issues as racial segregation, and the Vietnam War.

Robbins, L. (1996). *Censorship and the American library: The American Library Association's response to threats to intellectual freedom, 1939-1969.* Westport, CT: Greenwood Press. The freedom to read became a guiding principal of American librarianship during this period. Yet the ALA also frequently failed in its defense of this principle during this same period.

Robbins, L. (2000). *The dismissal of Miss Ruth Brown: Civil rights, censorship and the American library.* Norman, OK: University of Oklahoma Press. Brown was the town librarian at Bartlesville (OK) Public Library for thirty years when she was fired in 1950 ostensibly for refusing to remove books and periodicals from her library's collection. But Miss Brown's case was far more complex than a "simple" censorship issue.

Samek, T. (2001). *Intellectual freedom and social responsibility in American librarianship, 1967-1974.* Jeffferson, NC: McFarland. An examination of some crucial years in which librarians engaged in the purism of intellectual freedom versus libraries as agents of social change.

Schuman, P. G. (Ed.). (1976). *Social responsibilities and libraries: A Library Journal/School Library Journal selection.* New York: R.R. Bowker. These articles originally appeared in the pages of *Library Journal* and *School Library Journal.*

Venturella, K. (Ed.). (1998). *Poor people and library services.* Jefferson, NC: McFarland. The ALA has a "Policy on Library Services to Poor People" which recognizes the barriers that poverty presents to information access. This collection of essays describes the barriers and what can be done to eliminate them

> History does not refer merely, or even principally, to the past. On the contrary, the great force of history comes from the fact that we carry it within us, are unconsciously controlled by it in many ways, and history is literally **present** in all that we do. James Baldwin

Eclectic Reading for Informed Citizens: A Personal List

> It is certain, in any case, that ignorance, allied with power, is the most ferocious enemy justice can have. James Baldwin

Ansary, T. (2002). *West of Kabul, east of New York: An Afghan American story.* New York: Farrar, Strauss, Giroux. After September 11, Ansary wrote a moving email that went around the world, and then he wrote this exquisite little book about his bicultural American life.

Boyer, R. O. & Morais, H. (1975). *Labor's untold story.* (3rd ed.). New York: United Electrical Radio and Machine Workers. Opinionated for sure, but never a dull moment in this history of unions distributed by one of the most activist unions of them all.

Bradsher, Keith. (2002). *High and mighty: SUVs—the world's most dangerous vehicles and how they got that way.* New York: Public Affairs. Dangerous, gas-guzzling, polluting, egoistic vehicles—so why are they so popular and so destructive? Bradsher tells all and automakers apparently can't stand it.

Brown, D. (1970). *Bury my heart at Wounded Knee: An Indian history of the American west.* New York: Holt, Reinhart, Winston. Gut-wrenching history of the making of America.

Gobodo-Madikizela, P. (2003). *A human being died that night: A South African story of forgiveness.* Boston: Houghton-Mifflin. The author, a clinical psychologist who was a member of the Truth and Reconciliation Commission, had a series of encounters with Eugene de Kock, the commanding officer of the apartheid state's death squads, which caused her to write this extraordinary examination of guilt, self-examination, good, evil, and human transformation.

Hedges, C. (2002). *War is a force that gives us meaning.* New York: Public Affairs. This *New York Times* war correspondent has seen it firsthand and explodes the "myth of war" in our times.

Hertsgaard, M. (2002). *The eagle's shadow: Why America fascinates and infuriates the world.* New York: Farrar, Strauss & Giroux. Full of information that you won't get on the nightly news, but goes a long way in *explaining* the nightly news.

Korten, D. C. (1995). *When corporations rule the world.* West Hartford, CT: Kumarian Press. A primer on why all those young people are out in force against the World Bank, the International Monetary Fund, and international corporate globalization.

Levitas, D. (2002). *The terrorist next door: The militia movement and the radical right.* New York: Thomas Dunne Books/St. Martin's Press. Not all fundamentalist enemies of American-style democracy hail from the Middle East. Levitas traces and documents the origins of the Posse Comitatus, its deep roots in the racial history of the U.S., and the places they lead.

McChesney, R. W. (1999). *Rich media, poor democracy: Communications policy in dubious times.* Urbana: University of Illinois Press. The subject is the takeover by corporations of the media of the US and the resulting loss of a diverse press. The FCC, under Michael Powell, is poised to make media even more concentrated, which is an urgent concern for librarians and the public, but currently is an issue off the radar screen.

Moore, M. (2001). *Stupid white men and other sorry excuses for the state of the nation.* New York: Regan. You'll laugh 'til you cry.

Robinson, R. (2000). *The debt: What America owes to blacks.* New York: Dutton. This is basic reading to begin to understand the call for reparations for the effects, still present, of African-American enslavement and Jim Crow.

Roy, A. *Power politics.* (2001). Cambridge, MA: South End Press. The author of the prize-winning novel, *The God of Small Things,* is a peace and justice activist in her native India. In this book she writes about the destruction of the life of millions of Indians by a gigantic system of dams and government duplicity. She also explains her strong anti-war convictions.

Schriffin, A. (2000). *The business of books: How international conglomerates took over publishing and changed the way we read.* New York: Verso. Shriffin, the former head of Pantheon, writes about the concentration of book publishing into a few hands and the price the reading public pays for the new "bottom line" values that exist.

Walker, A. (1988). *Living by the word: Selected writings 1973-1987.* New York: Harcourt Brace Jovanovich. This activist writer's essays beautifully communicate her personal and political sensibilities.

Zinn, H. (1980). *A people's history of the United States.* New York: Harper & Row. The latest edition of this book marks the sale of 1,000,000 copies. It's U.S. history from the point of view of the "losers."

> If you don't know history, it's as if you were born yesterday. Howard Zinn

[This is a revised and expanded version of Ann Sparanese's bibliography supplementing her article, "Activist Librarianship: Heritage or Heresy." It appeared together with that article in *Progressive Librarian,* No. 22, Summer 2003.]

The Myth of the Neutral Professional

By Robert Jensen

The rules of life in modern authoritarian and totalitarian states are clear. The state—which represents the interests of a particular set of elites—governs through a combination of coercion and violence that typically is quite brutal, and propaganda that typically is heavy-handed. In that formula, intellectuals have a clear role: serve the state by articulating values and describing social, political, and economic forces in a fashion consistent with state power and its ideology. To the degree one does that, one will be rewarded. The Soviet Union was perhaps the paradigm case of this kind of system.

In a contemporary liberal, pluralist, capitalist democracy such as the United States, things are more complex. The state—which represents the interests of a particular group of elites—still maintains a monopoly on violence and uses it when necessary to maintain control. But because of the nature of the system and the advances made by popular movements in the past century, the state cannot rule simply by force or crude propaganda. Those who rule also realize that one advantage of a relatively open society is that it fosters a dynamic, creative intellectual climate that produces innovation. To elites, that innovation is desirable in certain realms (especially the sciences, both pure and applied) but potentially dangerous in other realms (especially the humanities and social sciences). How to encourage innovation in one arena but discourage it in the other? This requires the state to maximize social control through a more complex management of ideology and the institutions that reproduce and transmit that ideology.

In short, the liberal, pluralist, and democratic features of the system are constantly in tension with capitalism and the state (which typically serves the interests of capital). As Alex Carey (1998) put it: "The twentieth century has been characterized by three developments of great political importance: the growth of democracy, the growth of corporate power, and the growth of corporate propaganda as a means of protecting corporate power against democracy" (p. 18).

But propaganda in a liberal, pluralist, democratic system is not achieved by direct state control of the institutions in which intellectual work is done and through which ideas are transmitted. Intellectuals in the contemporary United States do not face the crude choices (subordinate yourself to the state or risk serious punishment) that intellectuals in more authoritarian states face. While dissident intellectuals in the United States are not always treated well—they may risk not being able to find permanent employment in an officially recognized institution, for example—they are not at this point in history routinely subject to serious consequences. However, while this is true for those from the more privileged sectors of society, there are contemporary examples of harsh treatment of those considered outsiders. Sami Al-Arian, a tenured Palestinian computer science professor at the University of South Florida, was vilified in the mass media and fired in December 2001 for his political views (see American Muslim Voice and United Faculty of Florida). In July 2007, Ward Churchill, a tenured professor of Ethnic Studies, was fired by the University of Colorado for what he considered exercising his right to freedom of speech (see Ward Churchill Solidarity Network).

In a liberal, pluralist, capitalist democracy, the elites in the state and the corporation must adopt a strategy different from authoritarian states to contain the potential threat from intellectuals. Elites need intellectuals in some arenas to innovate, while in other arenas they need intellectuals to articulate values and accounts of reality that will support the system of concentrated power. But given the substantial freedoms in place in the society, allowing intellectuals to have the time and resources to pursue the truly independent, critical inquiry needed for innovation poses a risk: what if some of those intellectuals engage in that work and come to a critique of the concentration of power that elites want to maintain? What if, instead of articulating values in support of that power, intellectuals articulate other values? Even worse, what if those intellectuals use their privilege not only to talk about such things but to engage in political activity to change the nature of the system and the distribution of power?

In short: in a system in which intellectuals can't easily be killed or shipped off to the gulag when they get feisty, how can they be kept in line?

The Neutral Professional

Enter the myth of the neutral professional, as a way to neutralize professionals. Here I will shift from the term "intellectual" to "professional," because I want to focus on how the myth of neutrality works in specific occupational groups: journalists, university professors, and librarians, three of the most important intellectual positions in this society.

In the political and philosophical sense in which I use the term here, neutrality is impossible. In any situation, there exists a distribution of power. Overtly endorsing or contesting that distribution are, of course, political choices; such positions are not neutral. But to take no explicit position by claiming to be neutral is also a political choice, particularly when one is given the resources that make it easy to evaluate the consequences of that distribution of power and potentially affect its distribution.

Myles Horton, the founder of the Highlander Folk School in Tennessee and a legendary figure in progressive organizing and adult education, is one of many who have critiqued the act of claiming neutrality, which he described as "an immoral act." Neutrality, he said, is "a code word for the existing system. It has nothing to do with anything but agreeing to what is and will always be—that's what neutrality is. Neutrality is just following the crowd. Neutrality is just being what the system asks us to be" (Horton & Freire, 1990, p.102).

Similarly, South African Archbishop Desmond Tutu has said that neutrality is choosing the side of the oppressor: "If you are in a situation where an elephant is sitting on the tail of a mouse and you say, 'Oh no, no, no, I am neutral,' the mouse is not going to appreciate your neutrality" (Reuters, 2004).

This same insight lies behind the title of Howard Zinn's political/intellectual memoir, *You Can't Be Neutral on a Moving Train* (1994). If a train is moving down the track, one can't plop down in a car that is part of that train and pretend to be sitting still; one is moving with the train. Likewise, a society is moving in a certain direction—power is distributed in a certain way, leading to certain kinds of institutions and relationships, which distribute the resources of the society in certain ways. We can't pretend that by sitting still—by claming to be neutral—we can avoid accountability for our roles (which will vary according to people's place in the system). A claim to neutrality means simply that one isn't taking a position on that distribution of power and its consequences, which is a passive acceptance of the existing distribution. That is a political choice.

In the contemporary United States, professionals who want to be taken seriously in the mainstream political/intellectual culture (and have a chance at the status that comes with that) are encouraged to accept and replicate the dominant ideology. Two key tenets of that ideology are the claims of (1) the benevolence of the United States in foreign policy (the notion that the United States, alone among nations in history, pursues a policy rooted in a desire to spread freedom and democracy) and (2) the naturalness of capitalism (the notion that capitalism is not only the most efficient system, but the only sane and moral economic system). At the same time, those same professionals are encouraged to be politically neutral, but within this narrow framework that takes the legitimacy of state power and corporate power as a given. In practice, this means one is supposed to present material that takes no explicit position on which policies should be implemented in the existing system, but one is not supposed to step back and ask whether that existing system itself is coherent or moral.

 I am not arguing that people who work within, and accept, the dominant ideology are by definition wrong or corrupt; reasonable people can disagree about how best to understand and analyze complex systems. My point is simply that it is not a position of neutrality. Those of us who routinely critique the dominant view are political; that is, the politics we have come to hold certainly has an effect on the conclusions we reach—but no more and no less than people who don't critique. That is not to say that journalism, university teaching, or library work is nothing but the imposition of one's political predispositions on reporting/writing, research/teaching, or acquisitions/program design, but simply to observe that everyone has a politics that affects their intellectual work. The appropriate question isn't "Are you political?" but instead should be "Can you defend the conclusions you reach?" It is interesting that the criticism I have received in my university career for "being biased" or "politicizing the classroom" almost never includes a substantive critique of my ideas or my teaching. It appears to be sufficient to point out that I deviate from the conventional wisdom, from which the conclusion can be drawn that I am bad.

 To return to the train metaphor: When we ride on trains, we typically conform to the system. The trains run on a certain schedule to certain destinations. Once a person decides to take the train, it's understandable why we typically focus on working within that established framework. We don't tend to look at a schedule and then demand that the railway company route a train to a different location at a different time; in most cases it's easier to fit into the system than to buck it. But that keeps us from asking important questions: should this train be on another schedule? Should these tracks be ripped up and laid elsewhere? Or, maybe, should we not be riding trains at all in favor of some other transportation system?

The Rules

My adult life has been spent in journalism and academia. In journalism, the rules of "objectivity" keep reporters and editors hemmed in and discourage examination of those big-picture questions. Central to that is most journalists' slavish reliance on "official sources"—those people in positions of some authority within the mainstream institutions. These people from government and the corporate sector are presumed to be credible sources and, hence, have great power to determine what will be a legitimate story and how it will be defined; they are news framers and shapers.

In university teaching, similar objectivity rules are in place, varying somewhat depending on the discipline. The primary vehicle for this has been importing the methodology from the physical sciences into the social sciences, in an attempt to give the study of humans and human institutions the imprimatur of "real" science. In such a system, political and moral choices are obscured by methodology.

The result is that both journalism and universities are, in general, overwhelmingly conservative spaces, in the sense that they function mostly to conserve the existing distribution of power. But because they also are liberal institutions (in the Enlightenment sense of adhering to broad values of free thought), they also allow critical inquiry that takes some people outside the consensus that favors for the existing order. In my experience in both kinds of institutions, universities tend to be slightly more open to critique because there is more original work done there, which requires less stringent controls.

This argument about neutrality, and the assessment of modern U.S. journalism and higher education, can be applied to libraries and librarians. I speak here not as an expert or insider, but as a patron and citizen, someone actively involved in political organizing and eager to see a dramatic expansion of political dialogue and activity in the United States. My views are rooted not only in my status as a fellow professional in an intellectual field, but as a political activist.

Librarians' Choices

Two areas where these issues clearly are relevant for librarians are acquisitions and programming. Given limited resources and physical space, no library can acquire all possible publications and display them in the same fashion. Obviously, choices are inevitable. Those choices should be made on sound professional grounds, just as should choices about what perspectives a journalist includes in a story or what material a professor includes in a course. These professionals are trained to evaluate the quality of a book, source, or theory, and should be free to use that training and exercise judgment. But we also should not ignore that all those decisions have a politics to them. That does not mean they are purely political judgments, but that political and moral values—and the judgments that flow from them—inevitably affect the judgments.

To echo the arguments above, the attempt to cast such judgments as neutral merely accepts the conventional wisdom and existing distribution of power. Take a simple example involving the common assumption in the United States that the capitalist economic system is the only rational and morally defensible way to organize an economy. There can be, and often is, much debate about how to structure and administer a capitalist economy, but the system itself is rarely contested, despite centuries of resistance to capitalism around the world and considerable intellectual work underlying that resistance. Now, imagine that a librarian wants to produce a display of the library's resources on economics to encourage patrons to think about the subject. In many libraries such a display would include no critiques of capitalism, but simply literature that takes capitalism as a given. Such a display that ignores critical material likely would produce no controversy (except perhaps a few complaints from anti-capitalists about the absence of critique, who could easily be dismissed as cranks). It is unlikely that school boards or city councils would take up the issue of the obvious bias against socialism and other non-capitalist economic systems. Consider what might happen if a librarian charged with this task actually produced a display that carefully balanced the amount of material from as many different perspectives as s/he could identify. In many places, that display would be denounced for its "obvious" socialist politics. Now, imagine that a librarian, observing the way in which Americans are systematically kept from being exposed to anticapitalist ideas in the schools and mass media, decides to organize materials that compensate for that societal failure by emphasizing critiques of capitalism. That librarian could be guaranteed not only criticism and charges of political bias, but likely disciplinary action.

My point is simply that all of those decisions have a political dimension, which is unavoidable. My concern here is not which one is the right decision, but that the librarian whose display is in line with the conventional wisdom likely will escape criticism while any other choices will raise questions about "politicizing" what should be a professional decision. Unfortunately, this neutrality game will derail rather than foster serious discussion of the issues.

Programming is another important issue for librarians. In an increasingly depoliticized society in which there is less and less noncommercialized public space, it is crucial to claim as many venues as possible for public political interaction. We live in an odd time, when proliferating mass media channels flood us with more and more political talk, but there are few places where people can actually engage in politics as participants, not spectators. Libraries remain one of the few common spaces in the society where people come to engage ideas, and hence they are crucial sites where people looking for such engagement can find it, and where others can be encouraged to engage. Part of that can be accomplished by simply making space available. But librarians also can create opportunities for dialogue. Can that be done neutrally? The same analysis offered for the issue of acquisitions applies here. A professional librarian would make a judgment about what kind of programming is most needed in the community. While such programming shouldn't be politically partisan, in the sense of advocating for only one viewpoint, the choices involved will be informed by political decisions.

In all of these situations, the question isn't whether one is neutral, but whether one is truly independent from control and allowed to pursue free and open inquiry. In a healthy society, professionals would be given that independence—not just in theory but in practice—and out of the many choices that varied professionals would make, we could expect a rich cultural conversation and an engaged political dialogue.

The ideology of political neutrality, unfortunately, keeps professionals such as journalists, teachers, and librarians—as well as citizens—from understanding the relationship between power and the professions. Any claim to such neutrality is illusory; there is no neutral ground on which to stand anywhere in the world. Rather than bemoan that fact, I believe we should embrace it and acknowledge that it is the source of intellectual, political, and moral struggle and progress. If we take seriously this claim, then all people, no matter what their position, would have to articulate and defend the values and assumptions on which their claims are made. The other option is intellectual stagnation and political decline.

Works Cited

American Muslim Voice. Dr. Sami Al-Arian's case. Retrieved August 23, 2007 from: http://www.amuslimvoice.org/html/sami_al-arian_s_case.html

Carey, A. (1998). Taking the risk out of democracy: Corporate propaganda versus freedom and liberty. Urbana, IL: University of Illinois Press.

Horton, M. & Freire, P. (1990). We make the road by walking: Conversations on education and social change. Philadelphia: Temple University Press.

United Faculty of Florida. On the termination of a controversial professor. Retrieved August 23, 2007 from: http://w3.usf.edu/~uff/AlArian/

Ward Churchill Solidarity Network. Retrieved August 23, 2007 from: http://www.wardchurchill.net/

Reuters. (2004, March 17). Tutu chides Bush on oversimplifying U.S. terror war.

Zinn, H. (1994). You can't be neutral on a moving train: A personal history of our times. Boston: Beacon Press.

["The Myth of the Neutral Professional" originally appeared in *Progressive Librarian*, No. 24, Winter 2004. It is an edited version of a talk delivered to the Texas Library Association annual conference, San Antonio, March 19, 2004.]

Information Criticism: Where is It?

By Jack Andersen

Roughly speaking, one may say that the practitioners of literary theory are the literary critics; that is, those reviewing and critiquing works of fiction. But where, one may ask, are the critics of the functionality and legitimacy of knowledge organization systems? That is, for instance, bibliographies, classification systems, thesauri, encyclopedias, and search engines—all systems that in some way or another mediate the recorded part of society and culture. Such knowledge organization systems are also the professional tools of librarians. Due to this fact, we should expect that librarians have a lot to say about the roles and doings of these systems in the mediation of society and culture, but it is hard within the public arena to trace and hear the critical voices of librarians grappling with knowledge organization systems. We are used to reading and hearing the voices of cultural critics, social critics, and literary critics debating social and cultural issues— the kinds of criticism with well-established histories and adherents that exist in society. Jürgen Habermas (1962/1989) argued, in his book on the structural transformation of the bourgeois public sphere, that art criticism, social criticism, and literary criticism developed in public spaces like the coffee houses, saloons, and *tischgesellschaften* and became established schools of thought in written genres such as journals and newspapers. They became organized in the sense that criticism developed particular forms of communication in order to talk and write about social, political, and cultural issues in society. These particular modes of communication were maintained because of their appeal to and belief in rational discussion within the public sphere. The forms of communication and the public sphere were dialectical in nature. The public sphere constituted the place and space for particular forms of communication, while the particular forms of communication contributed to materialize and shape the public sphere. The notion of the bourgeois public sphere, as argued by Habermas (1962/1989), rested on the assumption that private citizens had equal and free access to the public sphere.

Public librarians embrace this notion in that they provide the general public with free access to "information" and thereby identify public libraries as part of the public sphere. This is a widely accepted truism, but we seldom hear librarians participate in the public sphere by means of writing or talking about issues that are concerned with or that threaten this supposedly free access to information.

Insofar that knowledge organization systems do play a role in our late modern society, we should expect that critics who knew this would have an interest in discussing such systems in the public sphere in order to reveal their social, political, and cultural consequences. But any explicit evidence of such a critic is yet rather invisible; that is, there remains to be developed a way of talking and writing about the role of knowledge organization systems in society and culture. For lack of a better name, I shall call such a person an information critic (or "public intellectual," see e.g. Weisser, 2002) and such an activity information criticism. Thus, in this paper I will argue for a conception of the librarian as an information critic. Starting with a critique of the lack of an information critic, I shall next pinpoint what such an information critic ought to look like, why it is needed and how the modern librarian may fulfill this task.

The Lack of an Information Critic:
The Lack of a Discipline

Librarians, and library and information studies in general, have always had a paradoxical self-understanding or ideology. On the one hand, they have seen themselves as promoters of, for instance, democracy, free and public access to information, civil courage and literacy. Black (2001) writes that

> *Public* librarians are especially keen to stress a natural correlation, as they see it, between their historic mission to democratize the dissemination of knowledge and the widening of access that the digitalization of information promises to bring about (p. 64; author's emphasis).

But the apparent lack of active and critical librarians implies that they cannot be seen as advocates of democracy because democracy as a historical category demands constant analysis and critique in order to be evolving and stable. Democracy is not a given condition, no matter how much access to information citizens have.

On the other hand, librarians have usually portrayed themselves as neutral agents in social and cultural communication. That is, librarians claim they make a difference, but are neutral with regard to how this difference is to be understood. One reason for invoking neutrality is, according to Agre (1995), the ideology of information, which

> serves to position librarianship as a neutral profession, in two senses: (1) librarians minimize their participation in the internal disputes of other communities; and (2) librarianship does not define itself in relation to the ideology of any particular community of patrons (p. 225).

If librarians would orient themselves to literatures and not information, Agre (1995) argues, they would be participating "in the internal disputes of other communities" as these make use of literatures and literature has a history and structure. As communities are constituted by literatures, they make use of literature with its history and structure in mind. By invoking "information," librarians transcend the history and structure of literatures and, therefore, librarians are unsullied by any requirement to define themselves "in relation to the ideology of any particular community of patrons." Could it be that, if librarians had to define themselves in relation to the ideology of particular communities, they would have to come out of the closet, becoming active agents, arguing for their position and ideology in relation to other ideologies?

What has contributed to this lofty, above-the-fray attitude among librarians? At this point we may take a look at what kind of "academic" tradition librarians are part of or the product of.

Library and information studies (LIS) is the field educating librarians. Broadly speaking, LIS is concerned with the production, distribution, and use of recorded knowledge, and the role of systems of organized knowledge in this activity. The way librarians think, talk, write, read, and understand their field is, of course, dependent on the hegemonic discourse in which they have been immersed during their education. That is, the prevailing discourse and schools of thought in library school forms librarians' ideology. To a large extent, the curricula and professional literature of LIS are today filled with technical and managerial language, and technical and managerial perspectives and writings. Thus, Pawley (2003) states that "...the prevailing style of LIS discourse uses techno-administrative language to address technical and managerial problems" (p. 426). This discourse style is widespread in scholarly LIS literature and it inhibits the field's ability to engage in exchanges with other academic disciplines. Cornelius (2003), among others, has commented on this when stating that,

> If LIS is to be recognized as a constituent member of, say, the social sciences, *then at some level we must use the same language and engage in the same theoretical debates*. It is not as if there has been no discussion of theory, method, and philosophy in the social sciences, or that such discussions are irrelevant to LIS (p. 612; emphasis added).

It is vital to LIS that it discursively connects with other academic fields as this paves the way for LIS to discuss its relation to, and role in, society and culture. Otherwise LIS becomes a free-floating field with no significance.

One main area of study in LIS is knowledge organization, an area filled with technical and managerial discourse. For instance, Andersen (2004) indicates the extent to which conference proceedings of the professional society for knowledge organization, the International Society for Knowledge Organization (ISKO), were dominated from the beginning of the conferences in 1990 by technical and practical issues. Recently, McIlwaine (2003) surveyed trends in knowledge organization research. These "trends" were largely technical, concerned with universal systems, mapping vocabularies, interoperability concerns, problems of bias, the Internet and search engines, resource discovery, thesauri, and visual representation. The survey clearly revealed that recent "trends" did not discuss or even inquire into the role of knowledge organization activities in society and culture. Knowledge organization cannot currently engage at this level simply because it has not yet developed a discourse which privileges the information needs of society and culture. It is the technical and managerial nature of the prevailing LIS discourse that makes it difficult to engage in public discourse. The lack of a socially engaged discourse results in what Andersen (2004) has referred to as an "informational surgery":

> If we only talk about it in the sense of referring to techniques, principles or methods we are in danger of presenting a picture of knowledge organization to students, researchers and the public that makes it look like what might be called an "informational surgery." That is, to view knowledge organization as an "intellectual cure" to society and its members and their interaction with systems of organized knowledge (pp. 218-219).

Such a view (i.e. "informational surgery") conceals every critical activity and removes attention away from the postulated significance of cultural and social needs.

Furthermore, textbooks like Harter (1986), Lancaster (2003), Large, Tedd & Hartley (2001), and Svenonius (2000) can be characterized as texts that solidify the use of technical and managerial language in LIS in the sense that they are basically how-to books, constantly referring to techniques, standards, principles, methods, and rules. If one's professional knowledge base has such texts at its foundation, no critical attitude is developed nor demanded because these textbooks do not question at all the role of information seeking or of knowledge organization systems in culture and society. They do not provide students with a language, an understanding, a knowledge that make them capable of participating in public discourse debating the functionality and legitimacy of these systems. These textbooks present, at worst, an illusion to students as they foster the impression that once a student masters such-and-such techniques and principles s/he will become indispensable to society. But one is indispensable only if others recognize the vital relationship between information service providers and users. No one cares or values whether a librarian has mastered particular techniques or principles, because the latter do not demonstrate that they themselves can make a difference in the life of the user. To "make a difference," to earn the status of being "indispensable" one needs an argument, and to argue is to be engaged in discourse. But by invoking such unengaged, technical language, LIS communicates an attitude to students that says: you do not have anything at stake; you are not a shareholder in this discourse simply because there is no discourse. Moreover, simply invoking techniques, standards, principles, and rules in order to legitimate a certain practice does not justify that practice, but rather hides behind the practice. Technique is not an identity, and if you do not have an identity, who can identify you in order to see if you make a difference, that you really are indispensable? I claim that such a recognized identity can only be achieved when participating and addressing issues within the context of a public sphere.

The above has pointed to the reasons behind why librarians do not see themselves, and consequently do not act, as information critics. The discourse of their disciplinary background, LIS, is concerned more with prescriptive issues rather than descriptive and analytic issues. During their training, librarians are not introduced to the theories, schools of thought, academic disciplines, and knowledge needed to engage in public discourse simply because LIS puts itself at a distance to society and culture through its technical and managerial discourse, although the field clearly does not hesitate from expounding on its own social and cultural significance. In that way, LIS has failed to produce information critics and, consequently, has also failed to develop a critical stance towards the objects of the discipline. In the following section I will argue for the education of a new information critic.

Towards an Information Critic

Society is the basic unit of knowledge organization. It has particular structures and spheres organized according to particular interests and activities (cf. Habermas, 1962/1989). These have been developed and shaped historically by a variety of human agents, and the structures and spheres have in turn shaped human activity. Thus, society consists of forms of organized and mediated knowledge, which is produced, distributed and used by humans.

SOCIETY AND ITS TEXTUAL MEDIATION

Social Organization

GENERATES

Religion, law, politics, science, economics, education, art, commerce, industry, and administration, which

GENERATE

Documents and information affiliated with institutions that support & maintain social structures, power and influence, which

GENERATES, produces & distributes, through a variety of genres:

books, articles, journals, laws, reports, memorandums, advertisements, newspapers, pamphlets, and different communicative situations, which

GENERATE

Knowledge organization systems

The depiction of text generation and organization within society in the outline above illustrates the forms and layers of organized and mediated knowledge in society. Although the figure is rather sketchy, it nevertheless shows that broader forms of organized knowledge constitute knowledge organization systems. The part of society that matters most to librarians is the one where knowledge or information, materialized in a variety of genres, is circulating, and what role knowledge organization systems have in relation to that circulation, which implies concern with the impact the circulation of knowledge has on society. If this is the case, it stands to reason that every analysis and critique of knowledge organization systems must be addressed, and understood, in relation to the forms and layers of organized knowledge in society. Librarians cannot offer a view of knowledge organization systems as isolated from society's total communication structures. The practice of librarianship needs to be conditioned by an understanding of how knowledge and documents are socially organized, because this social organization structures and influences the possibilities of knowledge organization systems. Acting as information critics, librarians should demonstrate what Warnick (2002) has called "critical literacy" which is,

> the ability to stand back from texts and view them critically as circulating within a larger social and textual context...It includes the capacity to look beneath the surface of discourse, to understand implicit ideologies and agendas... (p. 6).

Knowledge organization systems are also a kind of text, at least in the sense that they make use of textual features in order to represent and organize documents. That means they are also circulating "within a larger social and textual context." This social and textual context is what constitutes the functionality of knowledge organization systems as they are developed as a response to other organized textual activities in society. That is, information critics should be concerned with analyzing what kind of influence knowledge organization systems have in society, compared with other modes of organizing knowledge as expressed through textual activities. Information criticism needs to look beneath the layers of organized and mediated knowledge in society, the "surface of discourse" as Warnick (2002) calls it, in order to point to how particular knowledge organization systems work, and to see what motivates particular forms of organized knowledge. This should provide citizens with an understanding of how they might apply such systems when searching for knowledge or information, and of what they can expect of these knowledge organization systems, that is, what such systems can and cannot do.

Bibliographies provide an example here. The shift from print to electronic recording and distribution of knowledge has contributed to the detachment of bibliography from the larger history of documents and their role in society. This has caused a lack of awareness of the role of bibliography in society, as electronic databases seem to rest on an ideology of detachment that has supplanted the social grounding of bibliographies as documents with specific histories embedded in sociopolitical activities. If this activity of librarianship's past is no longer recognized and understood, it becomes difficult to conceptualize, much less argue for, the role of knowledge organization systems in general in society and culture.

Acting as information critics, librarians could contribute to the demystification of knowledge organization systems by participating in the public sphere, discussing and justifying why knowledge organization systems, and their functionality, should matter to the public. That is, librarianship must argue that these systems make a difference in society, and also show how they affect our professional and everyday activities. Librarians can and should actively do this by acting as critics of society's textually mediated communication structures.

One way of doing this could be to review and write about such systems in public magazines and newspapers, not only in the research literature. But, in order to do this, librarians need to develop a vocabulary, a discourse, that is not technical or managerial. Librarians as information critics need to address and discuss knowledge organization systems in light of what these do and do not do in people's lives. Such dialogue might contribute to the development of a popular conception that knowledge organization systems are an important—maybe even indispensable—part of society and culture. In so far as this is ever achieved, information critics can make an important contribution to the public's understanding of how the many knowledge organization activities going on in society operate and how these, in the long run, serve or suppress democratic purposes. This task would be, of course, conditioned by how knowledge organization activities are made visible to citizens whose social actions depend on access to knowledge materialized in documents. One way of making these visible is to talk about them in a public discourse (or sphere), to relate problems with knowledge organization systems directly to social and cultural problems. Only in this way can the wider public recognize the potential value and doings of knowledge organization systems. If people can see that the functionality of knowledge organization systems is connected with social and cultural issues, then they might come to understand why such systems perform as they do and, thereby, people might also come to see that like other kinds of information, knowledge organization systems are always grounded in particular ideologies. Having a particular ideology is not necessarily bad. It is not being conscious of the presence of ideology that constitutes a problem. The basic social and cultural responsibility of the information critic should be to inform society about the existence of the ideologies embedded within systems of knowledge.

All this is to say that analyzing knowledge organization systems is much more than merely "evaluating," for instance, databases or search engines and their technical capacities. It is to put the discussion of these entities into a critique of late-modern culture and society. This is not the first time such discussions have been called for. It has been suggested by Campbell (2002), for instance, in his review of Richard Smiraglia's book *The nature of "A Work": Implications for the organization of knowledge* (2001). Smiraglia argues that "the work" is a cultural construction. Campbell agrees with this, but emphasizes that it implies a greater sensitivity "...to the social processes that fabricate our conception of the 'work'" (p. 109). However, these processes are not, Campbell argues, articulated in catalogues. They are "...*to be found in, or derived from, closer and more comprehensive readings of social and cultural theory...*" (p.109; emphasis added). The call sounded by Campbell for readings of social and cultural theory in order to understand what knowledge organization systems such as catalogs articulate, that is, what catalogs do, represents another way of highlighting the significance of connecting studies into knowledge organization to broader theoretical horizons in order to raise consciousness about its activity.

The modern librarian envisioned as an information critic is sorely needed because systems of knowledge organization, in particular with the rise of the Internet, are part of our everyday life and human activities. This means that we are more than ever dependent on such systems, but at the same time we need critical insight into how such systems work and why. Otherwise, our dependence becomes one of slavery and not active participation. Therefore, critical analyses and criticisms of the tendency of these systems to pretend to act as naturalized tools are constantly needed, because they shape society and culture and, in turn, are shaped by society and culture. The modern librarian should be providing such a critique of bibliographies, catalogs, and encyclopedias, etc. because these are librarians' working tools, used daily when mediating society and culture. In this way we may consider the modern librarian as an information critic.

Conclusion

The above discussion has focused on information criticism and information critics. I have argued that librarians are not the primary ones to blame for not displaying a critical attitude towards knowledge organization systems. The root lies in their professional training: library and information science (LIS). This field cannot be characterized as a field that engages heavily with other, related academic disciplines concerning social and cultural issues. Therefore, LIS does not share a vocabulary with related disciplines. LIS has managed to create its own "metaphysical" discourse that tends to favor technical and managerial language use. Such language does not invite critical consciousness and analysis as it stands at a distance towards the objects it is talking about. Indeed, technical and managerial language often stands in opposition to basic human needs, and is more concerned with how to do things rather than describe and critically discuss how these things (i.e. knowledge organization systems) work or do not. In that sense, librarians cannot function as information critics because they are not in possession of the appropriate vocabulary. Librarians' discursive framework needs to change if they are to have a social and cultural significance, which librarians now and then proclaim they have. In other words, if librarians are to act as information critics, they have to engage in and address their professional problems in relation to public discourse. Only then can their proper significance be estimated and recognized.

Works Cited

Agre, P. E. (1995). Institutional circuitry: Thinking about the forms and uses of information. *Information Technology and Libraries*, 14(4), pp. 225-230.

Andersen, J. (2004). Analyzing the role of knowledge organization in scholarly communication: An inquiry into the intellectual foundation of knowledge organization. Copenhagen: Department of Information Studies, Royal School of Library and Information Science. (http://www.db.dk/dbi/samling/phd_dk.htm)

Black. A. (2001). The Victorian information society: surveillance, bureaucracy and public librarianship in nineteenth-century Britain. *The Information Society, 17*(1), pp.63-80.

Campbell, G. (2002). Review of The nature of "a work": Implications for the organization of knowledge by Richard P. Smiraglia. *Knowledge Organization,* 29(2), pp. 107-109.

Cornelius, I. (2003). Review of 'Current Theory in Library and Information Science,' issue of *Library Trends,* edited by William E McGrath. *Journal of Documentation, 59*(5), pp. 612-615. (http://firstmonday.org/issues/issue9_1/gerhart/index.html)

Habermas, J. (1989). *Structural transformation of the public sphere: An inquiry into a category of bourgeois society.* (T. Thomas Burger & F. Lawrence, Trans.) Cambridge: Polity Press. (Original work published 1962).

Harter, S. P. (1986). Online information retrieval: Concepts, principles and techniques. Orlando, FL: Academic Press.

Lancaster, F. W. (2003). *Indexing and abstracting in theory and practice.* (3rd ed.). London: The Library Association.

Large, A., Tedd, L. A. & Hartley, R. J. (2001). *Information seeking in the online age: Principles and practice.* München: K. G. Saur Verlag.

McIlwaine, I. C. (2003). Trends in knowledge organization research. *Knowledge Organization, 30*(2), pp. 75-86.

Pawley, C. (2003). Information literacy: a contradictory coupling. *Library Quarterly, 73*(4), pp. 422-452.

Svenonius, E. (2000). The intellectual foundation of information organization. Cambridge, MA: MIT Press.

Warnick, B. (2002). Critical literacy in a digital era: Technology, rhetoric and the public interest. Mahwah, NJ: Lawrence Erlbaum Associates.

Weisser, C. R. (2002). Moving beyond academic discourse: Composition studies and the public sphere. Carbondale: Southern Illinois University Press.

["Information Criticism: Where is It?" previously appeared in *Progressive Librarian*, No. 25, Summer, 2005.]

Towards Self-Reflection in Librarianship: What is Praxis?

By John J. Doherty

Praxis, in Marxist terms, refers to the process of applying theory through practice to develop more informed theory and practice, specifically as it relates to social change. The progressive ideal implied in this is obvious, and is of particular relevance to librarianship. Also, in responding to a challenge for the need of a more theoretical framework to inform library theory and practice, John M. Budd defines praxis for librarianship in progressive terms as "action that carries social and ethical implications and is not reduced to technical performance of tasks" (2003, p. 20). In saying this, however, Budd further agrees with Richard Bernstein's critique that the meaning of praxis has been watered down, in part, due to "an overenthusiastic affinity for technical matters and deference to technical expertise" (Budd, 2003, p. 20).

That there is a need for a clear idea of praxis in relation to librarianship is obvious when the profession's progressive roots are so clearly articulated in the Code of Ethics of the American Library Association:

> In a political system grounded in an informed citizenry we are members of a profession explicitly committed to intellectual freedom and the freedom of access to information. We have a special obligation to ensure the free flow of information and ideas to present and future generations. (American Library Association Council, 1995).

The goal of social transformation inherent to this statement should define much of library theory and practice. In some instances it does, in progressive terms that are reminiscent of educational philosopher Paulo Freire's "pedagogy of the oppressed." For example, information literacy instruction comes with the working assumption that information is a tool that "enables people to overcome their false perceptions of reality" (Freire, 1970, p. 86). Freire believes that "the transformation of thought to text requires the conscious consideration of one's social context" (Fiore and Elsasser, 1987, p. 89). In other words, the statement implies a theoretical framework to librarianship, namely that to librarians knowledge is a social construction and that there is no privileged constructor.

Yet, the technical rationalist tone of library literature has resulted in a technical rationalist outlook in the profession. Such an outlook is not only symptomatic of the profession's inferiority complex, but an example of transference. The true discussion in library literature ought to be on the praxis of librarianship, particularly within the "trademark pedagogy" (Kapitzke, 2003, p. 37) of librarianship, information literacy instruction. This requires attention to both reflection and direct action, and their relationship to each other. This paper, therefore, suggests that a model to follow can be found in educational literature, where there has been a similar tension between its progressive roots and a technical rationalist tone. By looking at how educators have developed the notion of praxis through critical self-reflection, in order to inform theory and practice, it is possible to come to terms with contrarian views in order to develop the critical theoretical framework essential to inform the changing practices of these difficult times in librarianship.

A Need for Critical Reflection

Librarians, however, are not very reflective practitioners. For example, Cushla Kapitzke indicts librarians for hiding behind their presumed impartiality. She criticizes this role as exempting school librarians specifically (and, I would argue, all librarians in general) from critical inquiry. I would further add that it also allows librarians to exempt themselves from the self-reflection necessary to praxis.

Freire's seminal 1970 work, *Pedagogy of the Oppressed*, argues for a transformative praxis, wherein education can be used to foster critical reflection and action in order to transform: the pedagogy of the oppressed, he states, is "an instrument for [the oppressed's] critical discovery that both they and their oppressors are manifestations of dehumanization" (Freire, 1970, p. 48). He goes on to say that the oppressed must see their reality as not closed, without an exit, but as something that can be transformed:

> Functionally, oppression is domesticating. To no longer be prey to its force, one must emerge from it and turn upon it. This can be done only by means of the praxis: reflection and action upon the world in order to transform it (Friere, 1970/1993, p. 51).

Henry Giroux speaks of a "notion of self-criticism [that] is essential to critical theory" (2003, p. 35). He calls into question the objectivity that positivism encourages: "critical theory contains a transcendent element in which critical thought becomes the precondition for human freedom. Rather than proclaiming a positivist notion of neutrality, critical theory openly takes sides in the interest of struggling for a better world" (Giroux, 2003, p. 37). Freire goes further, equating praxis with self-criticism: people will be truly critical only when "action encompasses a critical reflection which increasingly organizes their thinking and thus leads them to move from a purely naive knowledge of reality to a higher level, one which enables them to perceive the causes of reality" (Freire, 1970, p. 131).

Intrinsic to praxis, therefore, is reflection-in-action. Myles Horton intriguingly challenges people to act on their experiences (Horton and Freire, 1990, p. 146). If one examines the self-imposed objectivity of librarians in this light it is easy to lean towards Kapitzke's argument. For example, if one were to reflect on the "reference interview" (considered by many—myself included—to be a form of information literacy instruction) and the referrals made from it, one might begin to see the inherent privileging of information. The reference interview occurs usually when the librarian needs to learn more from her patron about his information need. The interaction is framed in a form of open-ended questions designed to clarify and draw out the needs of the patron and usually concludes with the librarian assisting the patron in meeting that need. Implicit in much of the description of the interview is that the librarian maintains her impartiality in the light of the request, using her skills to elicit enough data to make reasonable referrals.

In recent conversations I tried a little informal "self-reflection" with my colleagues; I was curious to discover the privilege inherent in these and other library transactions. What I discovered, mostly from digging, is that we tend to refer patrons to a core of information based on the Western cultural paradigm. This reminded me of what I previously wrote: that the resource selection process in libraries is hegemonic, depending as it does on privileged source lists and methods of collecting titles. On re-reading this piece, I was especially drawn to my argument that: "a recent survey of scientists and journal editors in developing countries discusses 'structural obstacles and subtle prejudices' that prevent them from sharing their research with the world" (Doherty, 1998, p. 404).

Dialog, or Reflection-in-Action

Carr and Kemmis (1986) suggest that educational practitioners have to be committed to self-critical reflection on their educational aims and values (p. 31). They go on to say that teachers should become more self-enlightened regarding their own world views and how these can distort and limit their professional roles in society. They suggest that praxis is just this—doing-action, or remaking the conditions of informed action by constantly reviewing such actions and the knowledge that so informs these actions (Carr and Kemmis, 1986, p. 33). If we replace teachers with librarians here, we could have a recommended course of action for our profession.

Freire speaks of the importance of a dialogic form of education in which pedagogy is developed and acted upon. He indicts the "banking" concept of education (in which instructors "deposit" information into learners, to later be "withdrawn" or parroted back in testing) as one that seeks to maintain the status quo—the oppressors seeking to maintain their position. Through a form of "problem-posing" education, the oppressed are encouraged to communicate, to become conscious of their own consciousness: "People teach each other, mediated by the world, by the cognizable objects which in banking education are 'owned' by the teacher" (Freire, 1970, p. 80). He goes on:

> Dialogue is a human phenomenon, of which the word is at the core. And in dialogue, there is no room for banking. The "dialogical man" is critical and knows that although it is within the power of humans to create and transform, in a concrete situation of alienation individuals may be impaired in the use of that power (Friere, 1970/1993, p. 91).

This dialectical notion argues that "observation cannot take the place of critical reflection and understanding" (Giroux, 2003, p. 38). Lather (1986), in calling for a praxis-oriented form of research, defines praxis as a "dialectical tension, the interactive, reciprocal shaping of theory and practice" (p. 258). As one reviews library literature and theory, one finds little in the way of critical reflection and understanding. In part, this is due to time constraints—the old argument of "I'm too busy to reflect." However, I would argue that it is also due to the fact that most librarians involved in the "trademark pedagogy" of information literacy instruction are not trained as either instructors or critical reflectors. Indeed, information literacy librarians would echo

Myles Horton: "the way to learn is to start something and learn as you go along" (Horton and Freire, 1990, p. 40).

However, adopting a form of library praxis would encourage reflection-in-action, informed by the theories and practices of the profession. One informs the other, and, therefore, one is equitable to the other. For example, it is safe to say that librarians have issues with scavenger or treasure hunts. Yet if one acknowledges this as a form of uncritical bias, it becomes increasingly obvious that there is a demand for in-house library orientations, unmet by librarians and thus filled by instructors through such hunts, which usually prove unsatisfactory to both students and library staff.

Recently I had the opportunity to engage in a dialogue with myself, my colleagues, and some campus peers on this very issue. A research article challenged me to critically rethink my attitude and bias against treasure hunts. It ultimately led me to try to find ways to engage students in learning about the library through a case-based, problem-based learning approach (Carder, Willingham, and Bibb, 2001). This method allows students to come to own their learning by giving them more control over the experience. We tried this with a class which was given one of four problems to resolve: researching occupations/careers, researching colleges, finding financial aid, or finding scholarships. In groups, these students brainstormed their problem-solving process, and then utilized resources (some of which were already pre-identified by the librarian) to resolve the issue at hand. We facilitated direction when called on, but this was meant to be a student-centered process. After 30 minutes, we reconvened, reported out, and wrapped up. Importantly, the librarian is not in control of the learning—the students were.

Peterson (2003) speaks of the progressive teacher as one who builds on her students' interests. To him however, the Freirian teacher does more: "She asks questions.... [e]ngaging children in reflective dialogue on topics of their interest" (Peterson, 2003, p. 365). In the previous library example, we did much of the same, challenging the concept of a library tour as an example of the Freirian concept of "banking" education. Just as Peterson notes in his examples, we preferred to look at the dialogic "problem posing" method—where "teachers and students both become actors in figuring out the world through a process of mutual communication" (2003, p. 366). Indeed, it was interesting that Peterson states that teachers themselves must undergo a transformative process; this is the challenge of a library form of praxis: "breaking the ideological chains of formal education, of past training, and the inertia of habit of past teaching" (2003, p. 367).

Transforming the Profession: Action Research

It is telling, when one examines the literature of information literacy instruction, that most of what is published could be categorized as action research. Beile (2003) takes library literature to task for a lack of disciplined inquiry. Most of it is comprised of program descriptions, bibliographies, and literature. In a generous moment, one could describe some of these program descriptions as a form of action research, wherein the practitioners (in this case, the librarians) are producing their own knowledge, sometimes in a dialectic of practice and theory.

In education, action research has been defined as "inquiry teachers undertake to understand and improve their own practice" (McCutcheon and Jung, 1990, p. 144). Action research, in other words, is focused on the practitioner, with the intent of self-reflection allowing for growth and change. The reason I am hesitant to completely ascribe action research as a category of library literature is the usual lack of self-reflection necessary to good action research.

A case in point would be my own co-authored paper on the development of a 3-credit information literacy class at Montana State University (Doherty, Hansen, and Kaya, 1999). This work was informed by the theories of Daniel Bell and the recommendations of the Boyer Commission on Educating Undergraduates in the Research University. It is clear on re-reading this work that the authors were, at first, learning as we went. Then, with the introduction of someone to the team with an interest in undergraduate education and the social forecasting of Bell, some theory began to inform the practice. We began to do what Gitlin (1990) refers to as identifying and examining normative truths (p. 448).

However, while we describe the development of our information literacy program in the light of such information, and imply some critical re-examination of our situation before fully completing the development, we are not very critical of the outcomes. While we do leave open many questions, especially those that arose from our review of our practices, it was unfortunate that most did not lead to a re-examination of those practices for continued improvement.

Conclusion: What is Praxis?

Recently some major voices in the library profession have argued that "[w]ithin library and information work there is a fairly long-standing antipathy toward 'theory'" (Budd, 2003, p. 20). I would concur with this statement: too much weight is given to the practical aspects of library practice at the cost of the theoretical. Yet, as Budd and others (Wiegand, 1999; Crowley, 1999) argue, it is only in a self-reflective praxis that librarians could critically engage with current theory. I would further add that practitioners could also actively begin to develop or transform that theory through critical reflection of their practice.

Praxis, therefore, in librarianship, is Freirian in outlook: "the action and reflection of men and women upon their world in order to transform it" (Freire, 1970, p. 79). It is very easy to assume that librarianship is a stable profession, wherein practice is stable, "less and less subject to surprise" (Schon, 1983, p. 60). Indeed, many of the textbooks of the profession encourage such thoughts. In practice, however, the average librarian is likely to speak of the ever-changing world of information, access to information, and ways of facilitating such access (Doherty, Hansen, and Kaya, 1999). Minus a grounded theory of librarianship or ways of developing a grounded theory, or even more specifically of information literacy instruction, librarians tend to fall back on technical, rationalist based methods even when ineffective.

Beile (2003) notes, for example, that much of the information literacy literature of the 80s and 90s focused on the "variety of strategies for orienting the students to the library and teaching them to use its resources and services more effectively" (p. 272). Few of these studies actually investigate the effects of information literacy (or, as she terms it, library instruction) on student learning. The academic library of the 21st century is a much different information environment than the majority of the academy has been used to. Librarians are bringing the library, and information literacy, into the academic curriculum—where the 21st century library is an integral part of the academic experience, and where students are asked to use it at the most appropriate moments to their research process, not just during the third week library tour.

Works Cited

American Library Association Council. (1995, June 28). American Library Association code of ethics. http://www.ala.org/ala/oif/statementspols/codeofethics/coehistory/codeofethics.pdf

Beile, P.M. (2003). Effectiveness of course-integrated and repeated library instruction on
library skills of education students." Journal of Educational Media & Library Sciences,
40(3), 271-7.

Budd, J. M. (2003). The library, praxis, and symbolic power. *Library Quarterly,* 73(1), 19-32.

Carder, L., Willingham, P. & Bibb, D. (2001). Case-based, problem-based learning: Information literacy for the real world." *Research Strategies,* 18(3), 181-90.

Carr, W. & Kemmis, S. (1986). Critical theory: The background. In *Becoming Critical: Education, knowledge, and action research* (pp. 131-33, 44). Philadelphia: Falmer Press.

Crowley, B. (1999). The control and direction of professional education. *Journal of the American Society for Information Science,* 50(12), 1127-35.

Doherty, J. J. (1998). The academic librarian and the hegemony of the canon. *Journal of*
Academic Librarianship, 24(5), 403-6.

Doherty, J. J., Hansen, M. A. & Kaya, K. K. (1999). Teaching information skills in the information age: The need for critical thinking. *Library Philosophy and Practice,* 1(2). Retreived August 17, 2007 from http://www.webpages.uidaho.edu/~mbolin/doherty.htm

Fiore, K. & Elsasser, N. (1987). Strangers no more: A liberatory literacy curriculum. In I. Shore, (Ed.), *Freire for the classroom: A sourcebook for liberatory teaching* (pp. 87-103). Portsmouth, NH: Heinemann.

Freire, P. (1993). *Pedagogy of the oppressed*. M. Bergman Ramos (Trans.) NY: Continuum. (Original work published 1970).

Giroux, H. A. (2003). Critical theory and educational practice. In A. Darder, M. Baltodano & R. D. Torres (Eds.), *The critical pedagogy reader* (pp. 27-56). New York: RouteledgeFalmer.

Gitlin, A. D. (1990). Educative research, voice, and school change. *Harvard Educational Review, 60*(4), 443-66.

Horton, M. & and Freire, P. (1990). *We make the road by walking: Conversations on education and social change*. B. Bell, J. Gaventa & J. Peters (Eds.). Philadelphia: Temple University Press.

Kapitzke, C. (2003). Information literacy: A positivist epistemology and a politics of outformation. *Educational Theory, 53*(1), 37-53.

Lather, P. (1986). Research as praxis. *Harvard Educational Review, 56*(3), 257-77.

McCutcheon, G. & Jung, B. (1990). Alternative practices on action research. *Theory Into Practice, 29*(3), 144-51.

Peterson, R. E. (2003). Teaching how to read the world and change it: Critical pedagogy in the intermediate grades. In A. Darder, M. Baltodano & R. D. Torres (Eds.), *The critical pedagogy reader* (pp. 365-87). New York: RouteledgeFalmer.

Schon, D. A. (1983). *The reflective practitioner: How professionals think in action*. New York: Basic Books.

Wiegand, W. A. (1999). Tunnel vision and blind spots: What the past tells us about the present; Reflections on the twentieth-century history of American librarianship. *Library Quarterly, 69*(1), 1-32.

["Towards Self-Reflection in Librarianship: What is Praxis?" previously appeared in *Progressive Librarian*, No. 26, Winter, 2005/2006].

The Professional is Political: Redefining the Social Role of Public Libraries

By Shiraz Durrani and Elizabeth Smallwood

Part 1: Librarians and Their Societies

The first question to consider is "what are libraries and information all about?" Let us take an experience from Kenya to answer this question. A library attendant lived in an area that produces coffee. When he went back to his rural home for holidays one year, he was asked by a number of peasants a simple question: "You work in a University library; you have information from the whole world around you. We want you to answer a simple question for us: we work from dawn to dusk growing coffee, right from tending little shoots, to weeding, to harvesting, to drying coffee beans, day after day, month after month, year after year. We hear that our coffee sells for thousands of pounds in London, yet we do not earn enough from our labor to buy our own coffee in local shops let alone feed and clothe our families. You tell us why not, you who have all the information at your finger tips, you tell us what happens to our coffee money?"

It was not as if the University library did not have information about coffee. It had one of the best agricultural libraries in Eastern Africa. The library's collection on coffee and other cash crops was rated world class. Yet the library was not equipped to answer these simple economic-political questions from local peasants.

Now the questions asked by the peasants are fundamental to the work of librarians. The local library did have adequate resources to meet the needs of its users. It is just that its services were not aimed at peasants and workers. More important, the information that was available was depoliticized. It took the agricultural world around it as a reality that could not be challenged. It failed to see the difference between the natural world in which the coffee was grown and the social world, which had created social relations, and which decided on who owned the land, how labor was remunerated and where the profits went. Nor was it considered necessary to understand and explain that reality, to examine its history and, perhaps to see the need to change that reality—as the Kenyan peasants were demanding.

Globalization and Effects on Libraries

The key issue then is to decide what the social role of librarians is. Should they take the social, economic, and political situation they find themselves in as "given" without understanding why and how we arrived at this situation? Is it their role to dig deeper into "facts" that are given to them by their social environment? Is it appropriate to see the role of librarians in the same light in which Marx saw the role of philosophers: "The philosophers have only interpreted the world, in various ways; the point is to change it" (1969, p.3).

But before we consider the question of librarians trying to change the world, we need to question whether they even interpret their worlds. A large number of professional libraries remain unconnected to the social and political reality around them. Their model of a "global library" is much like McDonald's restaurant outlets which serve the same product in every part of the world. While this approach may be a useful one in ensuring a standard level of service, and a useful model for maximizing profits for the McDonald's chain, it is disastrous for libraries if they want to root themselves in their local communities.

Librarians trained to run such global libraries take professional pride in being "neutral" in the social divide all around them. They thus become increasingly isolated from the majority of people in their local communities. Forces of corporate globalization then push them even further from their communities by offering to save staff time and mental effort by supplying pre-packaged "best sellers," guaranteed to meet the wants of 30% of the population (Audit Commission, 2002, Summary)—and to boost the profit margins of transnational publishers and booksellers. The success of their libraries is then judged by the number of such best sellers they manage to loan out. No critical questions are asked or answered here: what is a library all about? What is its social role? Who has the power to make key decisions, and on whose behalf are decisions made?

The "global library," then, is a standard library service that can be located in any geographical, social, or political situation, in any historical period, and still be expected to function normally as a "library." The global librarians who run these global libraries take pride in their non-political stand, in their "neutrality" in the social struggles going on all around them. They claim to be outside the social struggles taking place in their societies, somehow uplifted to a loftier position by their "professional" training. Their class position in their societies isolates them from the struggles of working people whose basic need for information is ignored by their libraries.

Corporate globalization can be described as the "process enabling financial and investment markets to operate internationally, largely as a result of deregulation and improved communications" ("Globalization," 2000). We do not intend here to go into details of what globalization is and how it affects libraries, as this has been dealt with adequately in a number of sources (see, for example, Sivanandan, 2003; International Federation of Library Associations, 2001.; Durrani, 2000). However, a key point that needs to be made is that not only are new technologies making it possible to rationalize tasks and work practices, but also make it necessary to change at a faster rate as technological progress is changing the world around them. At the same time, many traditional library tasks are increasingly being handed over to private companies, rather than being done in-house. As the whole local authority sector is redefined to become facilitators of service rather than direct providers, significant changes are on the way. Other areas of local authority work are also changing. For example, household waste collection is no longer done by local staff; schools and education are being removed from local authority control. It is inconceivable that libraries will continue existing as they now are for very long.

We are not arguing that all changes associated with globalization are necessarily bad. But we would like to see more librarians in Britain adopting the 10 point plan, proposed by Mark Rosenzweig and accepted by the Progressive Librarians Guild, supporting "democratic globalism" as opposed to corporate globalization:

> We shall oppose corporate globalization which, despite its claims, reinforces existing social, economic, cultural inequalities, and insist on a democratic globalism ..., which acknowledges the obligations of society to the individual and communities, and which prioritizes human values and needs over profits (Progressive Librarians Guild, 2000).

Iverson (1998/1999) explains how the politics of globalization affects libraries and their local communities. The inherently political role of librarians is clear:

As our global society becomes increasingly based on the commodity of information, power becomes increasingly focused and managed by those with access to information. Those without such access remain marginalized (Iverson, 1998/1999, p. 14).

However, Iverson notes, librarians often reject any stated political stance, seeing themselves as "neutral service providers," a position encouraged by their training:

> While librarians are trained to maintain an objective or neutral stance they are also expected to make decisions regarding "good" and "bad" materials. Unfortunately, they do not often recognize the inherent bias at work in making these decisions ... and generally regard the selection of materials as apolitical (Iverson, 1998/1999, p.15).

Few librarians have taken Muddiman's (2000) warning seriously:

> Exclusion thus challenges public agencies like the library service to produce policy and practice which will challenge social division and create a harmonious, diverse and more equal civil society where access to knowledge is a fundamental right of social citizenship. If the public library can rise to this challenge it might begin to successfully reinvigorate and reinvent itself. If it fails, then the public library too, like the poor and excluded communities it exists to serve, might find itself consigned to the margins of the "information" society in the twenty first century (p. 12).

Faced with a situation where libraries are blindly walking into extinction, it is important that those with conviction and commitment stand up for a new role of libraries in society—and actively practice this new role. In the world ruled by corporate globalization, it is too easy to drift along with the tide of "neutral" librarianship and do nothing to make libraries play a central role in liberating people, their cultures, and their economies from the privatized future that globalization has planned for them. This is not merely something that may happen in the future. It is already happening, as Rosenzweig (2005) points out:

> Trade ministers and negotiators alike are under increasing pressure to expose more services, like education, healthcare, culture, ... to the market powers of transnational corporations (n.p.).

The Myth of Neutrality

Thus the myth of the "neutral" librarian needs to be exploded. There is no way that librarians are or can be neutral in the social struggles of their societies. Every decision they make—how much to spend on books, which books to buy, what staff to appoint, how to manage services—is a reflection of their class position and their world outlook. What librarians do—and don't do—is not merely an academic question. It affects our understanding of our natural and social environment, which, taken in its totality, affects our world outlook, and affects what we think and what we do. It influences the minds of the younger generation and becomes the prevailing outlook of the adult world of tomorrow.

Manipulation of information, whether conscious or unconscious, is an important matter, not only in local life, but in international relations as well. Recent events have shown how misinformation can be used to generate popular support for wars of somewhat questionable legality, for example when the USA and Britain invaded Iraq, killing thousands of people in the quest for non-existent "weapons of mass destruction."

If librarians are involved in the world of information, then surely they have social responsibility to ensure that people get correct information. It is a matter of ethics that they challenge misinformation, particularly when this is used by a small, powerful clique to wage wars and kill people on false pretexts. But our average "professional" librarians are too "neutral"—or too scared—to challenge the hand that feeds them. At the very least, they need to make alternate views and opinions as freely available as they do the views of the ruling classes. But this is not what the "globalized librarian" is trained to do. However, many progressive librarians in USA are taking a stand for their and communities' information rights against the USA PATRIOT Act which seeks to take these rights away from people. Their example needs to be followed globally.

Two aspects of the job of a librarian are to collect and then disseminate information, in a relevant form and language, to all those who need the information. This gives librarians tremendous power as it is they who decide what material to acquire and how and when to disseminate it. However, the easy availability of information on the

Internet is fast changing their monopolistic role as it democratizes the flow of information.

Libraries and Society in Britain

There is often a time gap between the emergence of a new social reality and that reality being accepted in people's consciousness. Jacques (2004) refers to the gap between the perception and the reality:

> we still like to consider ourselves a global player, but in reality we are not: our pretensions are now more like pastiche, substance has been replaced by vacuity... Post-imperial Britain has become deeply parochial—yet we remain almost utterly oblivious of the fact (the liberal elite included) (n.p.).

Thus, lessons and reality of history are shut out from social consciousness by denying the reality of a new world where Britain is no longer the superpower ruling the world, where China is flexing its muscles to become the most powerful nation in the world. Yet most public libraries have very little relevant material in English from or about China—a fact reflected in the lack of awareness among people in general about that part of the world.

In a society that has sought to shut out the reality of a new globalized world, it is not surprising that its libraries have shut themselves in a dream world of presumed superiority and "professional" might. The fact that the library world has not come to grips with changes in British society is a reflection of British society as a whole not coming to grips its new reality.

Creating a People-Orientated Library Service

There is an urgent need to develop a library service that helps to create a new consciousness among people about their society and also about the position of their country in the context of the wider world. Only with such wider awareness can a people-orientated library service be built. Libraries cannot tell people what their "real role" is. They can only provide information to help people decide for themselves.

If there is going to be a true people-orientated library service, it is necessary that there be a clear understanding of social forces within which a particular library service operates. Librarians face a number of challenges today. Let us look at some of them:

The first need is for all librarians to investigate our society and our communities. Mao's recommendation, at a political level, is equally valid in the information field: "no investigation, no right to speak." It is important to understand working people's lives and struggles, be one of them, and then seek ways of creating a relevant library service.

In all societies with class divisions and class struggles, library services tend to be a service for elite by elite, providing a service to the dominating classes and their allies only. In situations like these, the process of liberating library service for those previously excluded is the key role of library workers and professionals. The challenge is to develop a service that is open to all, irrespective of class, race, gender, ability, age, sexual orientation, political beliefs, etc. Service needs to be inclusive, reaching out to all who are currently excluded. Yet this task is not easy. The very language of this struggle has been removed from the "mainstream" by government action. Thus class differences are not mentioned in government reports and policies; racism is hidden under the bland term "social exclusion" thereby not only removing the reality of racism from public mention, but resistance to it is also disguised as criminal acts or as "terrorism." No society can be serious about addressing social oppression and economic exploitation when it chooses not to admit the very existence of such.

If librarians are to build truly people-orientated libraries, they will need to stop operating in isolation from the progressive forces that are already struggling for liberation. It is thus important that we develop creative partnerships with progressive forces, such as trade unions, workers' and peasants' social, economic, and political organizations, youth groups etc. Alliances also need to be made with all those struggling against all forms of social oppression.

But before librarians reach that stage, they need to liberate their minds from the social, cultural, and political norms of class-divided society. Its information systems and education provide us with a one-sided view of life. We will need to see the whole picture and not just the aspects we are shown. In the library context, we will need to free ourselves from the commandments taught at traditional library schools. We will need to learn not to be "neutral" but, instead, take sides on behalf of those previously excluded in everything we do in order to build an "equal" library service.

As is the case in all social revolutions, there are no specific guide books on how to create a liberated, "open" library service. It is only the actual practice of learning from people that will provide a solution that is relevant to our particular social situation and will help us build libraries without walls.

But just learning from people is not enough. The next, and perhaps the most difficult, step is to turn our ideas into action. This is best done by empowering the excluded so that is they who decide how our resources are to be used and how our energies are spent. People themselves will then be the best judges of our success or failure. It is in putting these ideas into practice that a people-orientated, "open to all" service can be built.

Part 2: Public Libraries in England

Speaking to the Society of Chief Librarians in June 2004, the then Secretary of State for Culture, Media and Sport, Tessa Jowell, posed a number of challenges to the profession:

> This is a critical time for the future of public library services. Although for over 150 years, libraries have given pleasure and provided opportunities to learn, it is now time to ensure that libraries are relevant and inviting to future generations... the challenge is to generate new users... it is important to learn lessons about why people do not use libraries—only one third do, so how do libraries attract the other two thirds?

The Secretary of State made it clear that she wants change in public libraries. She explained what needs to happen so that libraries "become, once again, central points in local communities":

> But they can only take back this role if they consult local people, and put them in the driving seat. Not just once, but as a continuous dialogue ("Lend it," p.3).

This challenge, however, is not reflected in the initiatives that the Department of Media, Culture and Sport (DCMS) has taken, primarily through the Framework for the Future (F4F) program (see DCMS, 2003). The key development since the publication of F4F has been a program to put the key points of the Framework into practice, led by the Museum, Libraries and Archives Council (MLA). DCMS explains what the Framework is all about:

The DCMS has published a new strategic framework for the public library service: Framework for the Future. The policy document outlines the Government's long-term strategic vision for the role of public libraries. Its purpose is to help local and library authorities agree on the key objectives for the public library service with central government and local communities. The new strategy will enable libraries build on existing strengths and ensure they position themselves at the heart of the communities they serve (2003).

The Framework aims to do this by focusing on three key areas for libraries to develop: books, reading, and learning; digital citizenship; and community and civic values.

Recent developments led by MLA are positive moves in the right direction and go some way to make up for what some feel to be immense failures of the Framework (see for example, Durrani, 2003). This includes the "Fulfilling their potential" program which provides a useful guide to developing services for young people (The Reading Agency, 2004). Other developments include the redrafting of the Public Library Standards, with a focus on "impact measurement." It remains to be seen how far these efforts, taken as a whole, will challenge and change the foundations of the public library structure in Britain to ensure they meet the needs of all current and potential users of library service.

At the same time, unless issues mentioned above in Part 1 concerning commodification and globalization of information, "neutrality," and politics of information services are addressed on a national level, any changes that come about are likely to be partial and not able to address real problems.

Iverson (1998/1999), commenting on the important role that libraries have to play, raises concerns about their role:

> I would argue that their role should not be to act in "collusion with the forces which perpetuate disadvantage" (Harris, p. 75) but to redefine their role to assist in the establishment of a truly equitable society (p.19).

British librarians have generally ignored the fundamental issues about the role of public libraries that Iverson raises. The DCMS, through its enthusiastic endorsement of what is perceived by some to be the vision-less F4F, has failed to give leadership to a field desperate for change.

Part 3: The Merton Library Approach

It is in the context of the Secretary of State's challenge that developments in Merton Library & Heritage Service (MLHS) between 2000 and 2004 need to be seen. Change and development for relevant library service can only be made if a foundation for change has been created.

The following section considers how a changed environment made it possible for a project involving young people to become self-sustaining and, in so doing, create a new model of public library service that sought to place the needs of a particular community at its heart.

Creating Conditions for Change: Staffing Structure and Equalities

MLHS's new staffing structure, introduced in 2003, aimed to address some weaknesses identified in the earlier structure and promote an overall perspective of developing a relevant, needs-based service. The structure was split into two distinct "wings": Operations and Performance Management (O&PM) and Innovations and Development (I&D) in such a way that an equalities approach could be mainstreamed. This approach allowed the targeting of services to key sections of communities whose needs had not been fully met. The two-wings approach was expected to ensure that innovative services were initiated and developed in the I&D wing. The O&PM wing was expected to ensure that the day-to-day existing work of the libraries was carried on within a strong performance management culture, guided by policies developed in the I&D wing. Its role was also to ensure that new projects developed in the I&D wing would be nurtured and embedded as part of a mainstreamed service. The majority of the staff and resources were in the O&PM wing.

This approach was meant to resolve some of the contradictions identified in the service during the review begun in 1998. These included the contradictions between the needs of current users and potential users; between developing new services and maintaining current ones; and between resource allocation for new services and allocations to established services. Implicit in these contradictions was the key contradictions between new ideas and "traditional" ones; between staff and managers who support the "traditional" mode of service and those keen to develop a new model of service to meet new and unmet needs of current and potential users.

Two key requirements were considered essential for the success of the new approach. The first was the support and commitment from senior management in the library service, within the directorates of the local authority (e.g. the Directorate of Education, Leisure and Libraries in Merton), the local government authority as a whole (e.g. London Borough of Merton), and crucially, from Councillors (i.e. elected Councillors, also called Members).

The second requirement was the need to address, in a clear and appropriate manner, clear resistance to change from some senior and middle managers who did not support the change program and were unhappy about meeting the targets set out in the new program. Addressing such resistance is considered a key factor in ensuring that planned change takes place.

The existence of this resistance was identified as a key risk factor by the team from the Management Research Centre of the London Metropolitan University which had guided the service through the early period of change as part of a European Social Fund (ESF) supported change management and management development program.

Another area where the Service placed a great deal of emphasis was the need to have a policy approach in all its work. MLHS had a deficit of written policies, resulting in uneven practices between library sites. The aim of the policy approach was to address this deficit through the provision of policies that would, through effective performance management, ensure that there was uniformity in service delivery and resource use. At the same time the mainstreaming of equalities, with responsibility for equalities being transferred from the Equal Access Services cost center to individual libraries, was also to be governed by the policy and performance management approach, with the overall strategy being decided by the Libraries Senior Management Team.

The staffing structure recognized the fact that public libraries are at crossroads. The Audit Commission report, "Building Better Library Services" (2002) notes that while libraries have a place in people's hearts, they "are losing their place in people's lives." Libraries thus need to change if they are to be relevant to the communities they serve. MLHS believed that, for public libraries to be relevant, they needed to respond to needs within local communities and that they needed to be well placed to respond quickly to changing needs. This, it was realized, would necessarily involve moving away from the traditional "books based" approach to embrace a closer focus on informal learning through a wide variety of activities, providing information through a variety of means that would help people in many different aspects of their lives. Additionally, it would mean the recruitment of people with the types of skills not traditionally found in libraries, e.g. skills in working with youth.

Innovations Project Approach

In order to develop the needs-based approach, MLHS developed a number of strategic partnerships, enabling it to acquire new skills and enabling it to focus on what were key needs in Merton. The development of an innovations projects approach was thus a response to the need for change on several levels. It was recognized that the new staffing structure had to do the following:

- Respond to community needs
- Mainstream equalities
- Develop new skills within the Service

The aim of the innovations projects approach, therefore, was to take a targeted approach to outreach and develop library services based on need, which could then be embedded into mainstream service delivery. Such an approach was a key part of the new staffing structure, which had policy and performance management very much at its core.

The Innovations and Development wing was thus set up with key aims in mind:

- To mainstream equalities through a policy approach (the implementation of which would be performance managed by the Operations and Performance Management wing)
- To develop new services and reach out to marginalized groups of people via a program of "Innovations projects" targeted at specific groups
- To develop policies to support the mainstreaming of new services

- To ensure that managers and staff at all levels and sites take ownership and responsibility for services to all groups and communities in the catchment area of their site.

It was recognized that library services needed to develop and reach out to a wide range of people. At the same time, budget restrictions did not allow the Service to increase staffing. MLHS's response was to develop a number of partnerships, both within and without the Council, allowing it to target key groups of people, using dedicated staff, in developing new services to these groups. Staff were either wholly or partly paid for by the partners.

There was a shift in the service focus as part of the new staffing structure. The previous approach was to devote staff and resources towards Black and Minority Ethnic (BME) communities. However, this did not allow MLHS to develop services where the needs were greatest, and targeting services to BME communities, irrespective of needs, began to create unnecessary tensions among staff and communities.

The new focus was on age, as age was seen as the one equality issue that cuts across all groups. With a mainstreaming equalities approach the aim was to ensure that, within each age group, all equality aspects are addressed, e.g. race, disability, gender etc. By adopting this approach, the Service contributed to community cohesion and reduced the tensions that could exist when one community feels that resources are being directed away from its services to services for other communities in a narrow area. MLHS was therefore taking a needs-based approach to ensure that the limited resources were targeted to meet the needs of current and potential users.

Why the Innovations Projects Approach?

It was decided to use a project approach to bring about change and development in the Service. This approach has a number of positive aspects, for example:

- Allowed risk taking
- Could be stopped if programs did not meet requirements
- Could be operationalized if successful, thus becoming part of the "mainstream"

- Could develop new partnerships
- Could generate new resources
- Could help connect libraries to sections of the community not using the service before
- Could develop new skills in staff

Space does not permit consideration of all Innovation Projects, so there follows a focus one project only, Merton Sense, and an examination of its development.

Merton Innovations Project

This section focuses on one of the Innovations Projects, Merton Sense, as an example of how libraries can be community driven, rather than management driven, resulting in relevant, sustainable services responsive to community needs, as dictated by the community itself.

Recent reports on public libraries reveal declining usage of libraries by young people. New and creative ways of reaching them need to be found to attract them to use the service. Discussion with Merton's Youth Service revealed that young people in a less advantaged part of the borough were interested in exploring creative avenues not available in the local area. MLHS consulted with a group of young people, which revealed that they were interested in setting up and running their own project—a magazine by and for young people. MLHS, seeing this as an opportunity to connect with young people, worked with Merton Youth Service to provide the space, the information and communication technology (ICT) facilities, and the staff support needed to bring the magazine into being.

Merton Sense Leads the Way

The magazine was called *Merton Sense*, a title chosen by the young people themselves. Its aim was to connect young people, many of whom were from socially excluded groups, with their library service by actively engaging young people in designing the new service. The magazine was produced by them with financial and management support from the library service.

The first need was for to find a home for the magazine. Thus was created the "Youth Space" in the newly established Innovations Unit based at Mitcham Library. The Youth Service provided computers which set the group going. The young people themselves decided how they wanted the Youth Space decorated and what furniture they wanted.

The youth group consisted initially of about 12 young people, and grew to over 45 within the first year. This number has now grown to over 50 young people between 14 and 24 years old. The staff time that supported these young people in producing the magazine was very important to the project. Often, library staff spent additional time in the week working with group members on article writing and graphic design to make their pieces presentable for the magazine. *Merton Sense* works with some writers for whom English is a second language and believes that all young people have something to add, irrespective of their varying abilities. However, such young people benefited enormously from the input of staff who were able to advise them on writing in English. The qualitative nature of staff input enabled young people eventually to write without any assistance and, as such, was highly empowering. The success of *Merton Sense* would thus not have been possible without the commitment and input of MLHS staff.

The group produced the first issue of the quarterly *Merton Sense* in June 2003 with a print run of 1000 copies. A network of writers has been set up with different young people from around the world. Writers from Australia, Spain, and the USA have already published articles and plans are in place to encourage writers from Kenya, Pakistan, and Brazil to contribute articles. *Merton Sense* has empowered the young people of Merton to take action and put their views and ideas into a creative and enjoyable experience. The group has learned about writing styles, how to compile a magazine, cohesive teamwork, and working to reach deadlines.

Many of the young people involved with *Merton Sense* had never used the library service; some had never even been inside a library! As a result of MLHS initiating this project and introducing young, hitherto non users to the libraries, they are all now members of the library service and much more aware of the diverse resources available to them. Libraries have also been an invaluable resource for the group in terms of background information for writing and composing articles electronically and in book form.

A retired journalist who had worked for the BBC was a volunteer through the Lending Time Project, a British Home Office and DCMS-funded project whereby community members volunteer their services to local libraries in the aim of service development. This retired journalist offered support and advice for a while, from a professional prospective, on how to compile a magazine and provided invaluable experience on writing styles and skills, and on how to compose articles. His involvement was one example of how MLHS encouraged inter-generational work. The magazine has developed in many areas the skills of the young people involved. These include ICT, writing styles, and desktop publishing, thus improving their employability and further education options. The Welcome to Your Library Project, through its connections with Asylum Welcome, provided the group with young people who were new to the country and were from an asylum seeker or refugee background. The magazine gave them the opportunity to interact with other young people who may or may not have been from a similar background. For those not from a similar background, this experience helped to gain a greater understanding of refugee and asylum seeker issues.

Some Outcomes

The magazine connected many young people, some of whom had never used the library service before, to the libraries but perhaps *Merton Sense*'s greatest achievement is that it has empowered the local young community and brought a tremendous sense of community amongst the team and its readers.

Among achievements of the magazine, the following can be listed:

- Involves communities: A wide range of youth from different groups are able to speak not only to youth but to the wider community of Merton through the pages of *Merton Sense*. The young people are now maturely and openly tackling difficult subjects that are of interest to a wide group of people.
- Encourages reading: The use of the Internet and library resources to research articles is now commonplace among the young people involved in the project. *Merton Sense* itself is a literary product.

- Encourages learning: Participants have developed a wide range of new skills in a friendly, informal manner—these had not been provided by the formal educational sector. Besides the "job specific" learning of publishing skills such as ICT, layout, design, desktop publishing, writing styles, artwork, editorial work, etc, the young people have also developed a wide range of social and leadership skills, such as team working, people skills, and dealing with difficult issues in a mature manner,
- Shares information: *Merton Sense* speaks not only to young people, but to the whole community and keeps all informed of a wide range of issues from a youth perspective.
- Has the potential to be developed and adapted elsewhere: The model developed in Merton can work anywhere, with appropriate management support, resources and quality staff input and a trust in young people. In fact, the approach can also be adapted for other projects.

One of the key achievements for all team members, however, is the engagement in a learning process entirely driven by individual wishes to develop in particular areas. Examples include creative writing; journalism; language and communication skills; marketing and fundraising skills. Although informal learning is a key aspect of public libraries, without such a project it would have been extremely difficult for MLHS to offer such a range of relevant, community-driven learning opportunities. The opportunities afforded by this project have led to a number of achievements including:

- Two of *Merton Sense*'s writers were picked up by national magazines to write articles in a freelance capacity.
- Three of the young people involved are now studying towards a career in the media, with *Merton Sense* forming an important part of their portfolios and increasing their employability options.
- *Merton Sense*'s resident poet, Amie Russell, won a local poetry competition in which this project encouraged her to participate, and her work will now be published by Xpress in a new poetry anthology book.
- A number of young people have been awarded the Millennium Volunteer Award.

The Editor of *Merton Sense*, Duane Melius (2003), recalls what working on the magazine has meant for him:

> For the first time since I left school there was a valuable opportunity for me... From here *Merton Sense* began. It has been a joy to watch the birth of an idea and witness its refinement. Being part of *Merton Sense* gives me a sense of identity. It is heartening to realise there are agents in the community willing to give people like me a chance.

The magazine has gone from strength to strength and the initial print run has grown from 1000 to 15000. The magazine has now been renamed *Sense* and a website has been developed (http://www.sense.ik.com/).

Merton Sense: Strategic Issues and Lessons

There is no doubt that *Merton Sense* has played a key role in reconnecting the library service to a large number of young people in Merton. These include not only the ones directly involved in all aspect of producing and writing the magazine, but also hundreds on the mailing list, and those who get copies through libraries, youth clubs, schools, and in other ways. In the process, the library service was learning a new way of connecting with its potential users. The success of the project was recognized by the Office for Standards in Education (Ofsted) Youth Service inspection in 2004:

> At the *Merton Sense* Magazine group, young people took responsibility for project development, set challenging targets, evaluated their own progress and gained formal accreditation.

One of the areas recognized as requiring attention in local and public service is the need for innovation. The *Merton Sense* project can be seen as an example of an innovative service development, which at the same time helped to develop new skills in managers and staff.

Another issue that should be understood in the context of making organizational change is the need for effective leadership with a clear vision, commitment, and a strategy for ensuring success. In the case of Merton, this was certainly available during the period under review. *Merton Sense* also provides a very clear example of how service users can take total ownership of a new service if they are able to influence the direction of the service and are allowed to have control over it.

The key point is that an idea and a service should grip their imagination. The young people at *Merton Sense* are keen to keep the magazine going and are developing financial and political skills to meet the needs of this complex project. There are enough lessons here for local government managers to digest.

Conclusion

As societies develop, as new technologies create even more possibilities for growth, the communications and information sectors need constantly to develop in keeping with major changes in society. There is thus huge potential for developing services that meet the new needs of all people and it is quite possible for libraries to be at the center of this vastly changing world. Engaging with the traditional library commodity of information in a "non-traditional" way that responds to local contexts, via the involvement of local people in service design and development, will enable libraries to help bridge the gap between the information rich and the information poor. Libraries can thus play a part in better enabling local people to make informed decisions.

However, realizing this potential requires creativity, innovation, commitment, and vision on the part of service leaders. Effective leadership in the information field, therefore, is the key to making libraries places where different social, political, and economic forces in conflict can deposit their various views, experiences, knowledge, and world outlooks. By ensuring that this contradictory information and knowledge has an equal chance to be acquired, stored, heard, and understood, librarians and libraries can, perhaps, find a new social role for themselves. They will then have played a meaningful social role in creating more just and "equal" societies.

As custodians of information, librarians everywhere have a role to play in eliminating the root causes of poverty, illiteracy, unemployment, and inequality. It is no longer acceptable for libraries and librarians to refuse to acknowledge this social responsibility. The choice is simple: if the information profession does not acknowledge its social responsibility and act upon it, it will no longer have a social role. People will then develop alternative models of information and knowledge communication, which do meet their needs. There will then be no libraries as we know them today. The choice is ours to make—today.

Works Cited

Audit Commission. (2002, May 17). *Building better libraries: Learning from audit, inspection and research.* London: the Commission. Retrieved August 21, 2007 from: http://www.audit-commission.gov.uk/reports/AC-REPORT.asp?CatID=&ProdID=9D0A0DD1-3BF9-4c52-9112-67D520E7C0AB

Department of Culture, Media and Sport. (2003). *Framework for the future: Libraries, learning and information in the next decade.* London: DCMS. Retrieved August 21, 2007 from: http://www.culture.gov.uk/Reference_library/Publications/archive_2003/framework_future.htm

Durrani, S. (2000). Returning a stare: People's struggles for political and social inclusion. *Progressive Librarian*, No. 17, 3-34.

Durrani, S. (2003, March). Review of the Framework for the future. *Library and Information Update.*

Globalization. (2000). In *Collins English Dictionary* (5th ed.). Harper-Collins. Retrieved August 23, 2007 from http://dictionary.reverso.net/english-definitions/globalization

Harris, K. (1991). Information and social change in the 1990s. *International Journal of Information and Library Research, 3*(1), 75-85.

International Federation of Library Associations. (2001). The IFLA position on the World Trade Organization. Retrieved August 22, 2007 from http://www.ifla.org/III/clm/p1/wto-ifla.htm.

Iverson, S. (1998/99). Librarianship and resistance. *Progressive Librarian*, No.15, 14-19.

Jacques, M. (2004, August 21). Our problem with abroad: Britain has become a deeply parochial place in the era of globalisation. *The Guardian.* Retrieved August 23, 2007 from: http://www.guardian.co.uk/comment/story/0,,1287822,00.html

Jowell, T. (2004, June 21). Department of Culture, Media and Sports public libraries seminar. Quotes taken from notes by Alison Bramley for Society of Chief Librarians (SCL) members.

Lend it like Peckham! (2004, July-August). *Library and Information Update.*

Marx, Karl (1969). *Theses on Feuerbach.* (W. Lough, Trans.). From Marx/Engels Internet Archive. Retrieved August 23, 2007 from http://www.marxists.org/archive/marx/works/1845/theses/theses.pdf

Melius, D. (2003, August 13). Best thing I ever did. *Young People Now.* Retrieved August 23, 2007 from: http://www.ypnmagazine.com/news/index.cfm?fuseaction=full_news&ID=1684

Muddiman, D. (2000). Theories of social exclusion and the public library. In Muddiman, D. (Ed.), *Open to all? The public library and social exclusion.* The Council for Museums, Archives and Libraries, Working Paper, 3(1), 1-15.

Office for Standards in Education (Ofsted). (2004). Youth Service inspection in 2004. Reproduced as Appendix 2—Report following the inspection of Merton Youth Service by OFSTED. London: Ofsted.

Progressive Librarians Guild. (2000). Ten point program presented to the groups which met at the Vienna Conference of progressive librarians sponsored by **KRIBIBIE**. Available from: http://libr.org/plg/10-point.php.

The Reading Agency. (2004). *Fulfilling their potential: A national development programme for young people's library services.* Retrieved August 23, 2007 from: http://www.readingagency.org.uk/resources/children/fullfilling_potential/FulfillingTheirPotentialFullReport.pdf

Rosenzweig, M. (2005, February 19). Tell WTO trade negotiators: "Hands off services." Message posted on PLGNet-L listserv.

Sivanandan, A. (2003, March 12). Globalism's imperial war. *IRR News*. Retrieved August 23, 2007 from:
http://www.irr.org.uk/2003/march/ak000008.html

["The Professional is Political: Redefining the Social Role of Public Libraries" originally appeared in *Progressive Librarian*, No. 27, Summer 2006.]

The Hottest Place in Hell:
The Crisis of Neutrality in Contemporary Librarianship

By Joseph Good

"Mischiate sono a quel cattivo coro de li angeli che non furon ribelli nè fur fedeli a Dio, ma per sè fuoro."
("They intermingle with that wicked band of angels, not rebellious and not faithful to God, ho held themselves apart.")
Dante Alighieri, Divine Comedy, Inferno, Canto III, lines 37-39.

Contrary to common belief, the hottest places in hell, at least according to Dante Alighieri, are not, strictly speaking, reserved for those who remain neutral during times of crisis. That's not to say that the neutrally inclined get off easily in Dante's celestial paradigm, though. Dante places those who were neither for nor against God— "non furon ribelli né fur fedeli"—in a region all their own at the very mouth of hell. Their lot is particularly unenviable, as Dante's guide, Virgil, relates:

"Questi non hanno speranza di morte,
e la lor cieca vita è tanto bassa,
che 'nvidïosi son d'ogne altra sorte.
Fama di loro il mondo esser non lassa;
misericordia e giustizia li sdegna:
non ragioniam di lor, ma guarda e passa."

("They have no hope of death,
and their blind life is so abject
that they are envious of every other lot.
The world does not permit report of them.
Mercy and justice hold them in contempt.
Let us not speak of them – look and pass by.")

(Canto III, lines 46-65)

This sounds bad enough. It is therefore curious that history incorrectly attributes Dante as having consigned those guilty of neutrality to the hottest places in hell. Isn't "blind life," abjectness, and the envy of "every other lot" rather enough, considering what else lies writhing in Hell (according to Dante's witness)?

The fact is, the first connection between Dante and the "ultimate sin" of neutrality was made by President John F. Kennedy, Jr. Kennedy gave a speech on June 24, 1963, in Bonn, Germany, at the signing of the charter of the German Peace Corps. During that event, Kennedy made the following remark: "Dante once said that the hottest places in hell are reserved for those who in a period of moral crisis maintain their neutrality." Perhaps he was mistakenly thinking of the aforementioned lines 37-65 of *Canto III* in Dante's *Inferno*; or, perhaps Kennedy was confident that Dante, in his expansive view of human morality, had equated neutrality and the lack of moral initiative with the greatest sin a human being was capable of. After all, we should consider the times Kennedy was emerging from; Europe had been torn to shreds by two world wars in the past fifty years, the later of which had very nearly annihilated an entire people by the most horrific kind of genocide. Indeed, the Holocaust itself would never have been as efficient as it was without the willing, in fact the eager, participation of the police departments and para-militaries of the nations that became subordinate to the Third Reich, such as France (see, for example, Zuccotti, 1993; Zuccotti, 2000). The "neutrality" of the French and Germans who stood by while their friends and neighbors were shipped off to Buchenwald and Natzweiler-Struthof may well have been on Kennedy's mind as he stood on German soil and spoke that day in 1963.

So what precisely is meant by "neutral," anyway? Switzerland seems emblematic of "neutrality." Yet the Swiss government, in tandem with the Swiss banking system, conspired to smuggle millions of Deutschmarks of stolen Jewish money, in the form of gold bouillon, out of Nazi Germany during the height of the Holocaust (Eizenstat, 1998). All the while, Switzerland maintained an official political neutrality that enabled it to preserve the integrity of its borders throughout the war and escape war crimes prosecution afterwards. One might question how "neutral" this "neutrality" was if Switzerland was acting as a covert banking agent for the Nazi regime while remaining politically uncommitted on the international front. This begs the further question: is *this* the true face of neutrality? Did Switzerland's ostensive neutrality enable it to justify, on a moral level, financial dealings with the Nazi regime which ultimately contributed to the Holocaust? There is no escaping the definitiveness of Switzerland's neutrality, since it was their statement *to the world*; in the end, Switzerland may have been more "neutral" than anyone suspected.

For it truly seems that somewhere in neutrality lays the negation of moral responsibility. President Kennedy and Dante Alighieri both understood that there is an inherent moral duty in the virtuous citizen to take hold of everyday events, to shape and define them. In Dante's case, virtue was directly correlative with religious piety; in Kennedy's case, with participation in electoral democracy. In both cases, however, these men understood the dangers of allowing people to become neutral observers of history as it passed by. Kennedy perceived that such passivity led to uncontrollable downward spirals of political and social turmoil; Dante felt that moral indifference put a person's very soul at risk.

What are the social responsibilities of a librarian, vis-à-vis neutrality? The proposition that a librarian is responsible for neutrally communicating both sides of an issue, merely for the sake of ensuring that both sides are heard, seems fallacious, at best. Indeed, the very notion that both sides of an issue are inherently equal, and therefore entitled to an equal share of the public's attention, smacks of moral relativism. There's something more insidious, however, at work in such a practice. It is the perception that an idea must be given public hearing at all costs, regardless of its intrinsic worth. In such a case, the idea becomes secondary to the imperative to communicate the idea. The idea thereby loses any relevance in cultural or intellectual discourse.

Take, for instance, the argument presently raging over teaching intelligent design in America's classrooms. Gerald Graff (1992), a professor of English at the University of Illinois, wrote a book in which he advised that instructors should "teach the conflict" surrounding an academic issue so students could understand its context. The deeper, tacit notion here is that knowledge is neither inertly given nor merely a matter of personal opinion, but rather, established in the furnace of controversy.

The religious right took hold of Graff's idea and, in his own words, "hijacked it." The culture war that Graff sought to ameliorate has now, perversely, incorporated Graff's own idea as a weapon to be unleashed on the disciples of rational humanism (for further discussion, see Fish, 2005).

Graff's idea allows the religious right to divert attention from the relative merit of the idea they are advocating—in this case, intelligent design—and focus instead on theoretical notions of freedom and investigation. Truth and reality diverge; the idea itself is no longer the focus of interest. Rather, the notion that an issue (regardless of its individual merits) should be entitled to at least as much academic exposure as its contrary, takes center stage in lieu of real intellectual labor devoted to the idea itself.

What are the consequences of this practice? Simply, that any idea can be validated once attention is deflected from its claims and attached instead to some general truth or value that can be sanctimoniously affirmed. One is left not with an argument for an idea, but merely the quasi-religious certainty that the idea must be advocated for the public good. If this is what a librarian is reduced to—airing arguments merely because they exist in opposition to popular, moral, or ethical ideas—then the librarian is indeed peddling a set of hollow wares: ideas denuded of any moral or intellectual consequence.

The librarian's very space in the fabric of social and political discourse is threatened by the practice of neutrality. By offering neutral responses in the increasingly partisan cultural atmosphere, the librarian denies him or herself the opportunity to definitively reverse the tide of negative educational trends which has seen the diminishment of the influence of the library in American society. Neutral responses to the vital issues of gay marriage, African-American reparations, and affirmative action continually jeopardize the library's relevance in contemporary society. If the librarian cannot be motivated to take a stand on pressing social issues out of a sense of moral duty, certainly the librarian should break his or her neutrality in the name of self-interest.

Charles Knowles Bolton (1922) stated that "Ethics...have been inherent in his [sic] profession even when not expressed in a code" (p. 138). This moral/ethical focus of librarianship seems curiously gone astray these days. There is abundant discussion of professional standards and competencies, but little mention of an ethical basis for these standards. Without an ethical basis, these standards are fundamentally two-dimensional. It takes moral conviction to make a professional standard work; the habit of lackadaisically permitting any idea, no matter what its relative moral merit, to filter through the library to the patron, is an affront to the professional standards of the modern librarian.

Neutrality is the logical conclusion of moral relativism; it is the pose most naturally assumed as a result of an ethical regime whose standards are defined by transient events rather than by consistent and unswerving convictions. Moral relativism disavows any universally solid principles; it is a road to the hottest part of Hell with a stop in Auschwitz along the way. Mussolini's own words on the topic of moral relativism should serve as a clarion call to every librarian who presumes to sit on the fence and await the outcome of the sociopolitical conflict our public libraries now face:

> "Everything I have said and done in these last years is relativism by intuition...If relativism signifies contempt for fixed categories and men who claim to be the bearers of an objective, immortal truth...then there is nothing more relativistic than fascistic attitudes and activity." (Mussolini, 1924, pp. 374-377).

Works Cited

Bolton, Charles Knowles. (1922). The ethics of librarianship: A proposal for a revised code. *The Annals of the American Academy of Political and Social Science, 101,* pp. 138-46.

Eizenstat, S. (1998, March 23). Address to the United Jewish Appeal National Young Leadership Conference. Retrieved August 17, 2007 http://www.state.gov/www/policy_remarks/1998/980323_eizenstat_ngold.html

Fish, S. (2005). Academic cross-dressing: How intelligent design gets its arguments from the left. *Harpers, 311*(1867), pp. 70-2.

Graff, G. (1992). Beyond the culture wars: How teaching the conflict can revitalize American education. New York: W.W. Norton.

Mussolini, B. (1924). *Diuturna.* Milan: Imperia.

Zuccotti, S. (1993). *The holocaust, the French and the Jews.* New York: Basic Books.

Zuccotti, S. (2000). Under his very window: The Vatican and the holocaust in Italy. New Haven: Yale University Press.

["The Hottest Place in Hell" originally appeared in *Progressive Librarian,* Issue no. 28, Winter 2006/2007.]

About the Contributors

Jack Andersen, Ph.D, is an associate professor at the Royal School of Library and Information Science in Copenhagen, Denmark. He teaches courses on knowledge organization and sociology of science. His main research interest is knowledge organization approached from the perspectives of genre theory, medium theory, and social theory. Currently, Jack Andersen is investigating how to understand the function of digital libraries in contemporary digital culture. He is the author of several articles published in leading LIS-journals such as *Journal of Documentation*, *Library Quarterly*, and *Knowledge Organization*.

Dr. John J. Doherty is Librarian and Arts and Letters Resource Specialist Team Leader at Cline Library, Northern Arizona University. He recently completed his doctoral studies in Curriculum and Instruction. In the spirit of the arguments presented in the paper in this volume, his dissertation was framed in critical theory to explore the role of reference librarians in online learning environments.

Shiraz Durrani graduated from the University of East Africa and got his library qualifications from the University of Wales. He is a Fellow of the Chartered Institute of Library and Information Professionals (CILIP). He worked at the University of Nairobi Library from 1968 to 1984 when he moved to Britain. He worked at Hackney and Merton public libraries before taking up the post of Senior Lecturer in Information Management in the Department of Applied Social Sciences at the London Metropolitan University. *Information and Liberation: Writings on the Politics of Information and Librarianship* is the title of Shiraz's forthcoming book, to be published by Library Juice Press.

Joseph Good is a graduate of New College of Florida. He is currently pursuing a Ph.D. and is working on a critical study of the novels of Iris Murdoch. He has been employed as both an academic and a public librarian.

Sandy Iverson holds graduate degrees in Adult Education and Library and Information Science. She has been employed by almost every library sector at one time or another. Currently, Sandy is unemployed by choice and is wandering the world with her 13 year old daughter. See: http://travellingwithteen.blogspot.com.

Robert Jensen is a journalism professor at the University of Texas at Austin and board member of the Third Coast Activist Resource Center. His latest book is *Getting Off: Pornography and the End of Masculinity* (South End Press, 2007). Jensen is also the author of *The Heart of Whiteness: Race, Racism, and White Privilege* and *Citizens of the Empire: The Struggle to Claim Our Humanity* (both from City Lights Books), and *Writing Dissent: Taking Radical Ideas from the Margins to the Mainstream* (Peter Lang). He can be reached at rjensen@uts.cc.utexas.edu and his articles can be found online at http://uts.cc.utexas.edu/~rjensen/index.html.

Steven Joyce completed his M.L.I.S. at the University of Alberta, Canada in 1996. After various stints as a reference librarian, interlibrary loan specialist, and film classification officer, he went on to complete a Ph.D. in L.I.S. at The University of Western Ontario, Canada in 2003 where he examined the identity construction of lesbian, gay, and bisexual youth in part through their information practices. Currently, he works as a research analyst at MacEwan College, Canada where he also teaches degree-level courses in deviance and conformity, and the sociology of youth. He can be reached at joyces2@macewan.ca

Alison M. Lewis is a full-time faculty member teaching Library and Information Science at Drexel University's College of Information Science and Technology. She has previously held a number of professional positions in special, research, and academic libraries. She received her M.L.S. and M.A. degrees from Florida State University, and her Ph.D. from Temple University. Currently serving as the coordinator for ALA's Social Responsibilities Roundtable, she lives in Philadelphia with her husband and an undisclosed number of cats.

Peter McDonald is Dean of Library Services at Fresno State. A cofounder of the Progressive Librarians Guild, he has been active all his adult life in environmental, social justice and anti-war activities and organizations. Born in the tropics, he received his undergraduate degree at McGill University in Canada (during the Vietnam War) and his Masters at the University of Washington.

ABOUT THE CONTRIBUTORS

Mark C. Rosenzweig is one of the founders of the Progressive Librarians Guild (PLG) and of the journal *Progressive Librarian* (PL), and is currently on the Coordinating Committee of the PLG and on the editorial board of PL. He has been active in the American Library Association (ALA) as an elected Councilor-at large for many years and was one of the conveners of the Progressive Council Caucus. Mark has been involved, as well, with the ALA's Social Responsibilities Round Table (SRRT) on whose Action Council he has served several times. Having been both a public and academic librarian, Mark was, most recently, the Director of the Reference Center for Marxist Studies in New York City, a special collection and archive on American Communism. He is currently working in Zhenjiang, China.

Elizabeth Smallwood graduated from Manchester Metropolitan and Lancaster universities with a B.Ed (Hons) and MA respectively. She began work for Merton Library and Heritage Service in 1998 and completed her library management qualifications in 2002. She was the author, in early 2002, of *Communities Developing Communities*, a consideration of how a needs-based public library service can ensure that public libraries of the future continue to be relevant to local communities. Currently, she manages the newly built Raynes Park Library in south west London.

Ann Sparanese is head of adult and young adult services at the Englewood Public Library in New Jersey. A member of the Progressive Librarians Guild (PLG) and ALA's Social Responsibilities Roundtable (SRRT) and a former member of ALA Council, she has been active in movements for progressive social change and international solidarity all her adult life. She is her library's shop steward and a vice president in the Bergen County Central Trades & Labor Council. In 2003, she was the recipient of both the *New York Times* Librarian Award and ALA's Futas Catalyst for Change Award.

www.ingramcontent.com/pod-product-compliance
Lightning Source LLC
Chambersburg PA
CBHW070316240426
43661CB00057B/2667